DENISE W. GOODMAN

Congregational Fitness

Healthy Practices for Layfolk

Foreword by Hugh F. Halverstadt

An Alban Institute Publication

Library of Congress Catalog Card 00-104725
ISBN 1-56699-232-X

07   06   05   04   03   WP   2   3   4   5   6   7   8   9   10

Contents

Foreword

Many books on dealing with church conflict are addressed primarily to clergy and secondarily to lay church leaders. Helpfully, a layperson has written this book with the understanding that laity are the communal heart and mind of congregations. This book prescribes how a congregation-as-a-whole can transform the challenges of congregational conflicts into opportunities for spiritual well-being and faithful ministry.

Denise Goodman's basic idea is that laity are key to making their congregations "fit" for conflicts. This congregational fitness comes from engendering and training members in skills of listening, "unpacking" differences, tolerating ambiguity, seeing through false platitudes, and cleaning out inaccurate stories and old fights that burden a congregation's heritage. She coaches congregations for faith fighting. Her coaching accurately recognizes that, although pastors may come and go, lay members have longer tenure and thus a higher stake in making their congregation conflict friendly.

At the heart of Goodman's training exercises for a conflict-savvy congregation is her warning against commonly heard platitudes in conflicted congregations that encourage dishonesty, false peace, and overly simplistic thinking. She especially challenges the foolishness of comments such as, "We just have to move on and forget the past," and "Just get over it!" She rightly argues that when congregation members seek to cut off or suppress discussion of differences, they lose the chance to explore what is real and risk revictimizing those who have already been abused or slandered.

Instead, she coaches laity on how they can unpack differences among members and work through the issues in ways that plumb contending commitments in redeeming ways and that provide chances for imperfect contenders to apologize and to forgive one other in Christ. As congregations practice constructive responses and skills for unpacking conflicts, they become spiritually and emotionally immune from debilitating congregational illnesses such as burgeoning anxiety, repressive no-talk rules, emotional wounds from win/lose and lose/lose contests, and the wastefulness of replaying old conflicts in order to balance the score or avenge past defeats.

Laity in congregations not only suffer the longest from destructive church fights, but they possess the greatest power for preventing destructive church fights. A congregation's "ways of doing things" can effectively censor dirty fighting and sanction fair fighting among members. The congregation's power as stockholder can override the power of any malevolent stakeholders. Although the congregation as stockholder cannot resolve the issues, it can constrain stakeholders who would achieve partisan ends at the expense of the whole. Such congregational capacity to constrain dirty fighting and encourage fair fighting is of redemptive significance for laity and clergy alike. It is this congregational capacity that this book develops and uses to make congregations fit for dealing with differences. The book is a manual for Spirit-based, communal sanity.

Goodman is not an author with quick fixes. Not only does she prescribe a healthy regimen for congregational fitness in conflicts but she also describes a faith-filled plan for recovering from conflicts in unfit congregations. She tells of her own experience of healing from a devastating church conflict, and based on that experience outlines five steps that individual congregation members can take to live through rather than die from destructive church conflicts.

Congregations that take Goodman's advice to heart by training their members in the skills of unpacking their differences strengthen their outward ministries as well as their inward lives. Having become comfortable and competent in working through conflicts within, congregations can dare to "pick fair fights for shalom" in the public sector, bringing up controversial challenges posed by sexuality, genetics, nuclear power, and ecological threats that stalk human life today. They can engage in high-risk ministries, because they can constructively engage the ambiguities and complexities embedded in the social policies that are most urgent for human survival and public righteousness.

Although this book does not attempt to provide the structure and process resources needed to undertake such controversial ministries, it does provide the spiritual and behavioral foundations on which to build urgent efforts to retrieve realistically the world that God loves and calls us to sustain. By guiding congregations to become fit for conflicts, this book empowers congregations to become fit for greater faithfulness.

HUGH F. HALVERSTADT

Acknowledgments

I want to express my grateful appreciation to all who helped make this book possible:

- To the many fellow laypeople who, over the years, have shared with me their deepest feelings about both the joys and pains of lives centered in their congregations.

- To clergy friends who trusted me with their experiences and observations.

- To Bangor Theological Seminary, which encourages, nourishes, and celebrates the ministry of the laity as well as that of ordained clergy.

- To many friends who supported me through my own congregational experiences, and especially to Patricia Butler and Mary Ann Hoy, who continued to encourage me as I stumbled along this latest leg of my faith journey.

- To Beth Ann Gaede, who provided insightful editing and unwavering advocacy for the voice of laypeople.

- And especially to Lynn Bujnak and Peg Slater, who read drafts of this work, offered wise, caring counsel, and gave me the courage to trust my instincts.

Introduction

When serious conflict surfaces in a church, laypeople often are stunned. They feel frightened, angry, and helpless. They simply are not prepared. Many clergy have had some instruction in conflict management, but laypeople have seldom had such training. As a laywoman who has experienced her share of congregational conflict, I have come to appreciate our need to be better prepared and to honor our own perspectives. What follows is an exploration of the kinds of healthy habits and basic skills that we laypeople can develop to deal constructively with the conflict that will inevitably surface in our congregations. These skills and habits are aimed at preventing disagreements from becoming destructive.

WHY SHOULD LAY MEMBERS BE CONCERNED?

The most gifted pastor or rabbi cannot make us a fit congregation, a healthy one that regularly exercises good procedural and relational habits, if we laypeople do not get our act together. Similarly, we can minimize the damage that a troubled or incompetent minister might inflict if we have developed healthy habits of trust, mutual respect, and sound and fair processes for handling congregational problems.

We must be concerned because:

1. Ministers come and go, either through assignment by a denominational official or via normal career moves to larger churches or more challenging pastoral positions. Even a healthy pastoral term may not exceed five or six years. But the congregation remains.

2. Clergy cannot single-handedly manage conflict. In fact, if congregations (or at least lay leaders) are not prepared to deal in healthy ways with the problems and disagreements that all congregations face at one time or another, pastors cannot succeed in handling the conflict, no matter how well-trained they are. Developing healthy relational habits—sound, Gospel-driven ways in which we connect with each other—is every parishioner's responsibility, not just the pastor's.

3. Unresolved, destructive conflict consumes massive amounts of clergy and lay energy, leaving little or none for ministry. Embattled clergy and lay officers can become tentative and defensive, providing minimal leadership, lest they do or say something that will further rock an already pitching boat. "I think we're a church that walks on eggshells," a laywoman in one struggling congregation told me. "Everybody is afraid if they say something, another person will leave." If "eggshell-walking" persists, the pool of parishioners willing to volunteer to greet, usher, cook for church suppers, or manage the food cupboard dwindles as everyone hunkers down to avoid additional stress. Newly emerging needs for ministry such as day care, shelters for the homeless, or grief support go unmet, either because members are too exhausted from the conflict or because they fear that addressing such needs will further fuel the fire.

4. Congregations that are adept at conflict management will support and enhance their pastors' efforts. Clergy are likely to be more successful and less stressed in their ministry if their congregations are healthy. When laypeople take responsibility for healthy ways of resolving or coming to terms with differences, pastors can concentrate on ministry and are not likely to become scapegoats for other people's issues.

5. Congregations are on shaky ground when they become too focused on their pastors, according to some of my wise clergy friends. If laypeople assume that clergy are wholly responsible for congregational well-being, parishioners who are uneasy about problems and disputes among themselves may shift their anxiety and anger to the pastor, who becomes the unwitting scapegoat. The pastor ultimately may leave, but the problems remain. Conversely, parishioners blessed with a gifted pastor may rationalize that such a good minister will make everything right, and so they avoid dealing with issues that require laypeople to engage in open, sometimes painful, examination. Pastors and parishioners who recognize their shared responsibility for congregational fitness will be able to face and resolve problems together.

6. While most church-conflict authorities are clergy and most conflict-management training is directed at seminary students and ordained ministers, everyday laypeople are left with the residue of destructive conflict when their ministers move to another congregation. And in all too many congregations, the cycle of destructive conflict is repeated over and over, sometimes for decades because bad habits such as denial, power plays, and scapegoating become unexamined elements of congregational culture.

7. While there is an abundance of training and literature for professional conflict managers, the conflict may, by the time the experts are summoned, already have proved destructive to individuals and to that spirit that otherwise draws us together as the body of Christ. If outside counsel is needed, however, laypeople's healthy skills can enhance the chances that such a consultation will be successful. Ultimately, lay leaders will have to carry on when the consultant leaves.

8. Destructive congregational conflict is a negative witness to the larger community. This impression has both practical and theological implications. When a congregation gets the reputation that it is "always fighting," the news will reach newcomers by word of mouth, and they will likely steer clear. They will probably choose instead a congregation with a reputation for warmth, hospitality, and energy. Even more important is the truth in Peter Scholtes's hymn that proclaims, "And they'll know we are Christians by our love." That hymn is based on Christ's declaration, "By this everyone will know that you are my disciples, if you have love for one another" (John 13:35). What will others know about our discipleship or about Christ's Good News if all they see and hear is news about our repeated congregational battles? How can we witness to God's love and God's commandment that we love one another if the message we send to the community by our battles is that we continually hurt each other?

9. Clergy—whether they are parish pastors or judicatory officials—have a particular perspective. No matter how objective they try to be, they may not fully comprehend the problems that laypeople face when conflict erupts, especially if the conflict is with the pastor. And unless clergy have had extensive interim or afterpastor[1] experience, they may not recognize how deeply ingrained certain dysfunctional congregational behaviors may be or how unresolved congregational issues—papered over by temporary truces—may surface two or three pastorates in the future. A pastor may accept a call to serve a congregation and assume that whatever happened in the past has been put to rest. After all, things are going well, parishioners

appreciate the pastor's gifts, membership is growing, and new programs are succeeding. But no matter how dormant the congregation's underlying bad habits, they are likely to surface in a controversy under the leadership of a subsequent pastor, even if the successor is not directly involved in the issue.

This book will explore why churches are prone to conflict, the kinds of healthy habits laypeople can develop to handle conflict, and finally, healthy responses if the conflict reaches a crisis level. It is designed to be a fitness training manual for congregations to help them become "fit" for dealing with conflict in ways that are appropriate, healthy, and faithful to God's call to us to live in loving community and proclaim God's love to others.

It makes sense to develop these habits before major conflict occurs, when people find it easier to think and speak from the perspectives of faith and reason. Too often, when conflict erupts, we parishioners forget all about who and whose we are, about the spiritual values that called us to our faith community. Instead, we tend to apply secular methods of handling conflict—methods we use on our jobs or in a neighborhood dispute. And amid painful conflict, emotions are likely to rule the day unless parishioners intentionally employ healthy processes and have been equipped to implement them.

Before we begin a physical-fitness program, we are advised to check first with a physician, both to determine what aspects of our health may be problematic—high blood pressure, cholesterol, or blood sugar; excess weight; damaged knees; or aching backs—and to get prescriptions for diet, exercise, and perhaps medication. In the same way, this book examines congregational behaviors that become problematic and prescribes exercises to correct those conditions and lead us to congregational fitness.

Chapter 1

WHY WE FIGHT

I can't believe this is happening in a church. We're supposed to love each other.

And she's supposed to be such a good Christian. How could she do that?

I come to church to find some peace, but every time I turn around we're fighting.

How could a minister act like that? I could understand if it was a parishioner. But the minister?

Why do church people fight? That is the fundamental question underlying all of these comments and observations. The question leaves church members and even some clergy puzzled, frustrated, and increasingly troubled. After all, the church is supposed to be a place of love and peace and comfort and caring.

If those inside the church are puzzled, consider the reactions of those on the periphery—those who have never gone to church and those who have been turned off by what they have seen or experienced in churches. Too often all this fighting conveys a message absolutely contrary to the one we are called to share, the one in which we proclaim by our behavior as well as by our words that God's love and grace are endless and available to everyone.

In his book *Managing Church Conflict*, Hugh Halverstadt, professor of ministry at McCormick Theological Seminary in Chicago, suggests some basic explanations for the reality that churches often become battlegrounds. He points out that spiritual commitments and faith understandings are both central to one's psychological identity and highly inflammable. So when we disagree, we fear that our core identities are at risk. When our identities are threatened, we are prone to fight or flee. Some of us fight first and then flee if we are losing the battle or if the fight becomes too stressful.

Halverstadt also talks about the "volatile gospel" as a precursor of potential conflict. Christ calls us to social and personal change, Halverstadt says, and that sets up an almost inevitable struggle between those committed to preserving the status quo and those who seek to be faithful to this call. Change can be exciting and liberating for those who are spiritually centered and have a handle on stress. But if we are anxious or troubled about our jobs, families, or finances, change can feel unsettling, even threatening.

We Are Volunteers

Finally, Halverstadt refers to the voluntary nature of the institutional church, "whose structures and processes permit and even entice unaccountable uses of power."[1] Churches are vulnerable to conflict because they lack the ability to impose sanctions which, in healthy families and workplaces, enforce some form of accountability. For example, the church cannot "ground" an irresponsible member, as a parent might restrict a teenager who defies a curfew. The church can't easily "demote" or block a pay raise for a member as a supervisor might discipline an employee.

In fact, careless discipline of a parishioner whom some may consider to be an unacceptable, disruptive antagonist may either be misdirected or inflame an already tense situation. Sometimes the people branded "antagonists" are simply the messengers, trying to warn fellow parishioners of simmering problems that need attention, and disciplining the messenger would be unjust. Even if congregants are behaving inappropriately, they are likely to have friends who will "choose sides" if harsh sanctions are meted out, and discipline will deepen the core conflict.

When action is taken in a congregation, sanctions often are unspoken and underground. The Amish are candid about ultimately shunning one who is judged to be an offense to the gathered community. But in mainstream congregations such shunning is unofficial, communicated through a grapevine, and unlikely to present the kind of open, healthy confrontation necessary for repentance, forgiveness, and reconciliation. When such "shadow shunning" is employed, the troublemakers who are allegedly promoting unrest and division are not held accountable. They receive no care from their pastor or from concerned parishioners, who might help them address personal issues that underlie their acting out. If the people who are assumed to be causing the trouble are in reality sounding a prophetic alarm that something is wrong, the congregation is allowed to remain in denial and those unofficially and unfairly accused of misbehavior never have an opportunity to clear themselves. They may ultimately quit the church, often carrying deep spiritual scars and leaving behind a still unhealthy, conflicted congregation.

PASTOR PROBLEMS

The situation is even more difficult if the one alleged to be irresponsible is the pastor or rabbi. On the one hand, the minister may become the unwitting and innocent scapegoat for congregational anxieties or the personal problems of some members. At their worst, parishioners who intentionally target pastors for serious injury or destruction are "clergy killers," according to G. Lloyd Rediger, a veteran pastor to pastors.[2] But Rediger also acknowledges the occasional "killer clergy" whose behavior is toxic to congregations.[3] Because laypeople are taught from early childhood to respect and even revere clergy, members may remain in denial about a pastor's destructive behavior.

For some people, the pastor is the representative of God or, at least, the conduit to God. If the pastor is the problem, they fear they will lose their connection to God, so they are reluctant even to consider that the pastor may be engaging in harmful behavior. Others place the clergy on pedestals. "Pastors don't lie," they assume, so no matter how far a pastor's statements deviate from what these members observe for themselves, they think the pastor must be right or that they must publicly support the pastor.

Even in the more hierarchical denominations, clergy are not necessarily held accountable for their actions. Day to day, clergy are mostly on their own. Certainly they meet periodically with vestries or church councils or sessions where lay authority is vested. But absent a major congregational uprising, such lay bodies are often hesitant to criticize or rein in a problem pastor. If problems with clergy reach a critical point, judicatory officials—a bishop, superintendent, or conference minister—may be summoned. But they have not witnessed the ongoing situation and often are at the mercy of conflicting versions of what has happened from two or more factions when the situation is far more complex than any side is able to articulate. In some denominational polities, the bishop, superintendent, or other judicatory head has little or no authority to discipline clergy unless major malfeasance—sexual or financial misconduct—is involved.

UNREALISTIC EXPECTATIONS

Another generic condition of churches and synagogues also makes them vulnerable to destructive conflict. Most people believe that the church, after all, should be the one place where brotherly and sisterly love prevail, where other cheeks are turned, where people are not judgmental, and where forgiveness overflows. Such simplistic expectations may explain why inevitable conflict within congregations is not confronted early and in a healthy manner but is instead allowed to fester and grow. These expectations are simplistic because they ignore another profound scriptural lesson—that we all are sinners and that, in answering God's call to justice, we are called to confront the sin of injustice, which unfortunately crops up in congregations as well as in the outside culture.

The reality is that while some churches excel in motivating members to engage in the kind of educational programs that nourish a maturing faith and spirituality, all too many adult church members are stuck with a kind of third-grade Sunday school theology. We have absorbed a few religious mottoes that urge us to "turn the other cheek" or admonish us to "judge not lest we be judged" or call us to "love thy neighbor." But often even these maxims are voiced or heard outside their biblical context. Further, we often avoid the tougher Gospel lessons about justice, standing with the oppressed and marginalized, and speaking the truth with love. We conveniently overlook Micah's reminder of what the Lord requires: "to do justice, and love kindness, and to walk humbly with your God" (Micah 6:86).

Congregations risk destructive conflict when parishioners interpret turning the other cheek to mean keeping silent about hurtful power struggles and manipulative behavior. We risk serious trouble when we focus only on speaking with love and ignore speaking the truth. Mature personal theology requires the tough discipline of keeping constantly in tension justice and humility, love and truth.

Halverstadt addresses this subject when he advises principals in a conflict to confront and rethink their own "gut theologies" before entering the management arena. "Rethinking gut theologies involves updating one's habitual, unexamined inner beliefs and ideas with Christian messages that incorporate these larger Christian perspectives," he says. For example, he notes, a "gut theology" motivated by the scriptural admonition that we should not be anxious about tomorrow, for tomorrow will take care of itself, may lead to the assumption that if we ignore conflict, things will work out. Updating this gut theology by a mature understanding of the Gospel involves understanding that Jesus consistently addressed conflict, rather than ignoring it. To "be reconciled, one to another," Halverstadt adds, may lead parishioners always to concede their point of view rather than do the hard work of genuine dialogue that may lead to genuine, rather than superficial, reconciliation.[4]

Finally, if the church is the place to which we expect to bring our troubles, we should not be shocked when those troubles sometimes surface in congregational conflicts. Sometimes, underlying a congregational dispute are frustrations transported from our jobs, families, or other outside settings. If we feel powerless or victimized at work, we may try to play out that frustration by inappropriately wielding power on a church board or committee. If we are experiencing painful marital problems, we may try to project our anger on the pastor or a visible lay leader. If we are being abused at work or at home, we may be supersensitive and interpret straight talk as a personal attack. We hope that membership and participation in a faith community will ultimately be a transforming experience. But church doors are not like Etch-a-Sketch slates, automatically erasing all our human flaws when we walk through them.

So here we are in church—dealing with issues that touch us most deeply, hearing a Gospel call that shakes up our conventional assumptions and disturbs our comfort zones. We are a group of volunteers without the disciplinary tools, available in other areas of our life, to hold each other accountable for our behavior. We are fallible folk with an unrealistically ideal view of what "church" should be. All too often, we are spiritual adolescents confronting difficult situations that require spiritual maturity.

Understanding why we fight is the first step in developing a congregational fitness regimen—perhaps akin to understanding the emotional triggers for overeating before embarking on a diet. We are not asked to deny the emotions, because they are real. When we are dieting, we are urged to understand those emotions and then learn and practice healthier alternative behaviors to deal with them. In the same way, we laypeople can acknowledge the emotions that sometimes prod us to behave badly and then learn and practice spiritually healthier alternatives that promote congregational fitness.

Questions for Reflection

1. What issues or developments in your congregational life make you uneasy? Why?

2. What are some of your "gut theologies" that might bear reexamining? How does your understanding of what it means to be "a Christian" affect the way you feel about and deal with disputes and conflict?

3. How might you reshape your "gut theologies" so that you will be more willing to deal with conflict and more effective? What resources (books, study groups, speakers, for example) do you need to accomplish this task?

4. What are some of the "volatile Gospel" issues that might ignite conflict in your congregation?

5. Have you ever brought your anger or frustration from your job or family to church? How did that play out in your behavior as a parishioner?

Chapter 2

CONFLICT:
NORMAL AND HEALTHY
OR DESTRUCTIVE?

Did you hear about the donnybrook at the church council meeting last night? They found a surplus in the mission fund, and everybody had a different idea of how to spend it. Jim wanted to send it to the hurricane victims, Sarah said the soup kitchen needed it, Mary thought it should go to the battered-spouses program, and Mike said the scout troop needs new tents. They finally reached some consensus and split it between the hurricane folks and the soup kitchen, but, wow, what a battle!

Workshop leaders frequently introduce sessions on conflict management by asking participants what comes to their minds when they hear the word "conflict." The responses are predictable—anger, tension, stress, avoidance, denial, discomfort, and unease—and mostly negative. Seldom does anyone respond with such words as "challenge" or "energizing" or "growth." And yet congregations that make every effort to avoid any conflict *(a)* almost always are unsuccessful and *(b)* do not grow spiritually or in their ministry. In large part because we cling to those immature "gut theologies" discussed in the previous chapter, we tend to view any conflict—from a difference of opinion to a dispute that requires some resolution—as spiritually unhealthy. "Turn the other cheek" becomes "turn off your sensitivity." "Judge not lest you be judged" turns off our ability to be discerning—to analyze issues thoughtfully.

"A congregational crisis is so frightening because the congregation instinctively senses that, if its Christian faith cannot be of help here, it cannot be of help anywhere," William H. Willimon, chapel dean and Christian ministry professor at Duke University, notes in his book *Preaching About Conflict in the Local Church.*[1]

Laypeople might be surprised, then, to learn that just about every authority on church conflict views low-level congregational conflict as normal and healthy. In fact, these experts say, churches with little or no conflict lack vitality. "[C]onflict occurs most often in congregations in which there is a deep commitment to the church," Willimon says. "People only fight over what is important to them." He adds, "Of course, not all church fights are over issues of theological substance, but all church fights are potentially revelatory of what is important to the combatants."[2]

"It is not possible for a church to be tension-free while being simultaneously faithful to all aspects of the Law and the Gospel," advises Speed Leas in *Moving Your Church Through Conflict.*[3] "We can expect normal conflict wherever normally functioning persons interact," G. Lloyd Rediger agrees in *Clergy Killers.*[4]

So if we layfolk are normally functioning people seeking to be faithful to the Law and the Gospel, conflict of some sort is not only inevitable, but necessary for our spiritual growth. Take the comment at the beginning of this chapter. Normally functioning people are attempting to be spiritually faithful by naming categories of concern for others which they believe deserve mission funding.

WHAT IS THE DIFFERENCE?

How do we distinguish healthy conflict from destructive conflict? And how can we avoid moving from one to the other? A good deal depends on how we approach issues and deal with them. In almost any congregation, we can expect to have problems, differences of opinion, disagreements, even personality clashes. Those are normal and mostly healthy. Consider the diversity within even a small congregation. It is made up of women and men, people of different ages, and probably in different economic situations, with varying political affiliations, church experiences, and theological views. Healthy congregations make wise use of such diversity. The adage that "two heads are better than one" has considerable merit. In a mutually respectful atmosphere, people with different backgrounds, understandings, and experiences can produce some surprisingly innovative solutions or even new ministries.

Consider this simple problem:

The church budget has been stretched by unusual expenses this year. We are expecting an unusually cold winter, and heating costs have risen. We can solve this problem by (*a*) scheduling some extra fund-raising suppers to pay the additional heating costs, (*b*) moving worship into the smaller, easier-to-heat parish hall, or (*c*) suspending Sunday worship for the two coldest months. There likely will be some disagreement—some differences of opinion—about the solution to this problem. And if Bill and Carol always seem to antagonize each other and each opts for a different solution, we may experience the result of a personality clash. Bill would close the church for two months, while Carol insists on doing the suppers.

If we are careful to listen honestly and to respect each other, if we are not unduly stressed by hearing differences of opinion, chances are that we will solve this problem without seriously alienating anyone. We might even come up with an innovative solution—perhaps agreeing to worship with the congregation down the street for several Sundays and, in return, helping them with a painting project.

THE FEAR FACTOR

Problems constitute the lowest level of conflict in Speed Leas's conflict hierarchy—which moves to progressively more serious disputes. Problems are low-level conflict, he says, because fear is minimal.[5] But what happens if fear of conflict surrounds the most simple problem? It is likely to escalate to a disagreement, a contest, a flight-or-fight choice, or even an intractable situation. Healthy congregations have a good handle on fear. In these churches, fear at the problem level is minimal because the congregations have successfully solved problems before. They know how to approach problems and have some confidence that they can resolve them without going to war. Unhealthy congregations have little or no history of successful problem-solving, so every time a problem emerges, they fear it will lead to painful, damaging conflict. That fear, in turn, drives up the anxiety level and, ultimately, the stakes. What might have been calmly discussed and resolved triggers instead anger and a lack of thoughtful listening. People are too occupied, scurrying to find a safe corner for themselves or trying to win what they perceive to be a battle, to genuinely hear and consider what others are saying. Often what turns healthy conflict into its unhealthy counterpart is some variation of those two extremes—either withdrawal and denial or insistence on winning at any cost.

There are several ways to make a molehill problem into a mountain conflict. One, obviously, is to view any disagreement or problem as a battle to be won. Another is to overfocus on the potentially dire consequences of any simple solution. However, it can be just as harmful to deny small problems, fearing they might spark hostilities. Refusing to deal with small problems seldom eliminates them. Instead, denial generally means the problem will escalate to a crisis stage, a point at which it cannot be ignored. I will have more to say later about avoidance, denial, and the no-talk rule.

Leas touches on another dynamic when he notes, in describing his hierarchy of conflict, that the severity increases as participants lose regard for each other. By the time the conflict reaches the "contest" level, participants are more interested in winning than in developing mutually comfortable solutions. By the fight-or-flight level, they want to hurt or get rid of opponents, he says, and at the highest "intractable solutions" level, opponents seek to destroy each other.[6]

So on the one hand, healthy conflicts can energize congregations. They can draw out the best thinking of parishioners and hone their interpersonal skills. Learning to agree to disagree, to hold a position without denigrating someone with an opposing one, and to be open to changing one's views after listening to new, relevant, and convincing information—these are important skills for lay members to develop. Like any exercise, they tend to keep us fit—fit to handle conflict in a healthy manner. Conflicts head down a dangerous slippery slope at the point where participants:

- Function in fear.
- Lose regard for others.
- Put winning ahead of any other goals and, eventually, seek to hurt or destroy opponents.

Conflict becomes destructive when it results in spiritual wounding, causing some to lose their faith or even to blame God for their pain. It is destructive when it fractures relationships, paralyzes a congregation, and prompts some people to question or even abandon their faith.

So after understanding why we fight, the next step for healthy congregations is to understand the difference between "good" conflict and destructive conflict—to appreciate and even to welcome the former as a sign that the Holy Spirit is nudging us to new spiritual growth, and to avoid the latter, which is hurtful and stifles responsible discipleship. The chapters that follow are designed to help laypeople spot danger areas and to develop skills to keep conflict in the healthy zone.

Questions for Reflection

1. In the last several years, what issues have arisen in your congregation that might be described as conflicts? Which were problems, which were disagreements, and which turned into battles? (It may be helpful to list them on a chalkboard or sheet of newsprint under these three categories.) What factors determined whether the issue was a problem, disagreement, or battle?

2. Think about a problem that your congregation faced and successfully resolved. How was it resolved? What behaviors led to the resolution? How did you feel, once agreement on a solution was reached?

3. Think about a problem that escalated to a more serious conflict in your congregation. How might it have been approached differently? Without naming individuals, what behaviors, fears, or feelings contributed to escalating the issue?

4. Think about a conflict that helped your congregation grow spiritually. How was that positive end achieved? What was the result?

Chapter 3

WHO ARE WE

AND

WHY ARE WE HERE?

I come to church for some peace, to get away from the pressures of work and family.

I come to be challenged, to grow spiritually.

I come to church because I want to be part of something bigger than myself, because I want to serve others.

I attend here because this is the church in town. People look up to me because I am a member of this church.

When congregational conflict erupts, attention immediately focuses on what divides people. Any previous sense of shared vision often gets lost in the emotional uproar. If we never talk about who we are as a faith community and what we believe is the mission of our church—the reason for our being together—conflict triggers a sense of chaos. Overt conflict may also expose significantly disparate assumptions about the identity of a faith community. Some may believe the congregation's major focus is on mission in the community; others believe its primary focus is deepening the spirituality of its members. Some may think the church reveres tradition, whereas others may think it is quite open to change. When all is going well, those differing assumptions may not seem to pose a problem. But when parishioners become anxious, the differing and often conflicting assumptions surface.

When I conducted a study of one dwindling congregation that was experiencing acute survival anxiety, I discovered that some members had distinctly different understandings of the church's identity. Some members thought their church was quite conservative; others saw it as fairly open and liberal. Still others were confused. "We have bounced from identity to identity. It's almost like, looking back on things, that we didn't make up our mind why we're here," one told me. "That's a problem," another remarked; "I think we've totally lost our identity as a church." Still another said, "I don't know who we are. Sometimes I think we're wandering in the wilderness." The "wilderness" is not a comfortable place to encounter conflict

When disputes surface, attentiveness to a shared vision can provide some stability and perspective. But too often congregations either pay lip service to the church's mission statement or ignore it altogether. It is simply an early paragraph in the church by-laws that hardly anyone bothers to read. Caught up in organizing church suppers, conducting stewardship campaigns, and teaching Sunday school, we seldom consider what is involved in shaping and maintaining our focus on a stated, shared, and frequently revisited mission statement—a statement that captures our common understanding of who we are as a gathered faith community.

Notice that I suggest the vision must be *shared, stated, and frequently revisited.* Parishioners may believe that their congregation has a clear and common understanding of its identity until conflict occurs and parishioners discover all manner of ideological and theological differences among themselves. During peaceful times, those differences may lie dormant, but they quickly take on sharp, divisive edges when conflict occurs. And if the congregation's mission has not been clearly stated, frequently proclaimed (perhaps as a part of worship liturgy), and regularly reviewed, it is likely to be forgotten or ignored when problems develop.

NEW GENERATIONS

At one time, perhaps before World War II, such a practice might have been less important. People were less mobile and more likely to live in one community for decades, if not for their entire lives. They often attended the church their parents attended and, as a result, grew up with a clear vision of their congregation's purpose. But circumstances have changed significantly. Many adults not only move away from home to begin their careers but also move from state to state in pursuit of improved job opportunities. And many now in their 30s or 40s enter churches with no previous religious training or experience. Recent emphasis on "welcoming church" strategies, such as printing the words to the Lord's Prayer and the doxology in worship bulletins, reflects an attempt to address the reality that an increasing number of adults enter churches without having learned and memorized these worship basics. Denominational loyalties are less important as people "shop" for a church or move to a community in which there is no church affiliated with the denomination in which they were raised. Veteran church consultants Roy M. Oswald and Speed Leas point to this reality when they note that "Baby Boomers have fewer institutional commitments than those who preceded them. They join what satisfies and drop out of that which does not."[1] Given the mobility and cultural mores of the baby boomers' offspring, the so-called Generation X, there is every reason to expect that they will continue this trend of shopping for a church. As a result, a Protestant congregation of 150 may well include people from Methodist, Episcopal, Presbyterian, Lutheran, Baptist, Disciples, Congregational, and even Roman Catholic backgrounds, for example, as well as those with no previous church affiliation.

We may assume that people come to church for the same reasons—to worship and to find a peaceful haven amid their increasingly anxious and stressful lives. But it is a safe bet that in most churches, rationales for involvement in the life of the congregation are both varied and potentially conflicting. The following are some of the most frequent explanations people may offer for attending a particular church:

- My parents and grandparents belonged to this church.
- I want to be part of a group that helps others.
- The church is an impressive and historic building.
- I am seeking a place of spiritual retreat and healing from the pressures of family and job.
- I want to be challenged to grow in my faith and spirituality.
- I want to meet people, make friends, and socialize.
- I want to be part of a faith community that takes stands for justice on issues of racism, sexism, classism, and homophobia.
- I am single [widowed, in a nuclear family far from my relatives] and look to the church as my surrogate family.
- Belonging to Church X will give me status in the community.
- I am frustrated at home or on my job and need a place to work out or act out my frustration.

- I feel powerless at home or at work. Perhaps I can become empowered or become a power at church.
- I want to fit in and be considered a good citizen. If I go to church, people in my community will respect me.
- I have a general sense that the church sets a moral tone for the community. I'm not very interested in the details of religion, but supporting the church just seems like a good thing to do.

WHEN EXPECTATIONS CLASH

It does not take a genius to recognize that some of these expectations or motivations can be at loggerheads with others. Those who seek spiritual solace and peace may resent spiritual challenges that provoke in them an inner sense of discomfort or even guilt. Those whose loyalty is primarily to the building may find the spiritual content irrelevant or even irritating. By the same token, those seeking spiritual peace or challenge may be irked by those whose primary focus is the building or sociability. Those primarily interested in the building want any extra funds to be spent on preserving it, while those interested in social action want to devote extra funds to a food cupboard, a homeless shelter, or a day-care center for the children of teenage mothers.

The power issue may be healthy or destructive, depending on motivation. A person who feels powerless on the outside may gain a healthy sense of being included, of being heard and helpful, in a faith community. Such empowerment within the congregation can be an important source of emotional and spiritual healing. But power will be misused and ultimately become destructive if it is wielded by someone with a need to dominate and control others. Social-action agendas are often unpopular with those seeking status. And, by the same token, social-action-oriented people have little patience with those who simply seek status in their church affiliation.

In large urban areas, it is possible for a church to have a narrowly focused vision. Such a vision may not be formally articulated but simply acknowledged from experience and reputation. When I inquire about churches in a new community, I may be told that First Parish Church is *the* church to attend, that Hope Methodist Church does a lot in the community, that Faith Lutheran Church sponsors a number of spirituality and study groups, and that First Baptist Church has a great Sunday school and young couples club. But few churches can survive with narrowly defined and sometimes spiritually bankrupt visions. Many would argue that all churches are called by the Gospel to have, as a friend of mine puts it, "very wide doors," to be inclusive rather than exclusive, to celebrate diversity rather than seek homogeneity. At the same time, a vision so bland that it appears to cover every potential need or want or personal outlook, including purely secular desires, will be neither faithful nor very helpful to spiritual seekers. For example, social status is not a legitimate expectation of a Christian faith community; moreover, such a view runs counter to the Gospel. Loyalty to a building without a hunger for spiritual nourishment is similarly problematic. Still, most congregations are composed of members with differing expectations and needs. If those multiple expectations and needs of parishioners are not openly acknowledged, destructive conflict is almost inevitable.

In his book *Faith Before Faithfulness*, H. William Gregory, United Church of Christ minister, addresses this issue when he explores "three doors to the one center," three prime motivations for joining and remaining in a church. Some, Gregory says, enter through the *spiritual door*, pursuing a spiritual journey, "a self-conscious pursuit of God." Others, hearing "the call of God in love for the suffering people of the world," enter through the *justice door*. Finally, those who pursue the caring community and find their religious experience in "belonging" enter through the *caring community door*.[2] Gregory affirms each door as spiritually valid. But he also recognizes potential tensions, even among those who have entered the church seeking a genuine connection to God, but from different perspectives. Those called by a spiritual hunger can become pietistic and dogmatic and fail to appreciate concerns for justice and the importance of relationships. Those seeking to "do justice" can similarly become self-righteous and chafe at emphasis on the mystery of God and the importance of fellowship. And, says Gregory, those seeking participation in a caring community often put security first, viewing justice pilgrims as a threat to harmony, and spiritual pilgrims as "too abstract to be of earthly good."

So the question becomes whether it is possible for parishioners to gather and discern among their differing expectations and priorities some common ground that enables them to articulate a faithful shared vision of the church that gives vitality to their life together as well as a level of comfort.

SHARING THE VISION

Mission statements are designed to stand the test of time. They often are composed of only a few sentences or paragraphs that state the timeless underlying principles upon which a congregation stands. Mission statements should be clear, concise faith statements, a kind of theological or spiritual bottom line.

In the workshops he conducts around the country, Stephen Gifford, former minister of evangelism for membership growth with the United Church of Christ, offers some warnings. "The church that thrives in the 21st century," Gifford declares, "will be the church which proclaims and lives its core values. . . . Where vision is well defined and embodied with integrity, God brings growth. Where vision is fuzzy and divided, God will not bring growth." Gifford's observation might apply as well to handling conflict. The church that proclaims and lives its core values, the church that has a well-defined vision embodied with integrity, will be better prepared to address conflict. Gifford suggests some exercises that clergy can use to clarify their own vision, exercises that should be just as useful for laypeople. For example, he suggests listing:

- A half-dozen key scriptural phrases or concepts that are most important to you.
- Five kinds of encounters Christ had (for example, sacramental, confrontational, healing, teaching).
- Old Testament themes related to God's realm; ways that God knows us and that we can know God.

Gifford asks two additional questions:

- Why do you believe? Not *what*, but *why*.
- What is your theological/spiritual/faith "bottom line"?

Parish consultant Lyle Schaller, in *The Interventionist*, has a similar take. Before congregations can grow spiritually and numerically, he maintains, they must discern their "central organizing principles." He offers a list of 43 such principles and suggests that many more could be added. His point is that until a congregation determines one or more central organizing principles, its clergy and lay efforts either will be stuck in

inertia or will ineffectively scatter in too many directions.[3] Discovering the
theological bottom line or central organizing principle is crucial because it
prompts us to examine how we can honor diversity without compromising
those things that are foundational to our faith. For example, a congregation
may allow wide leeway in personal beliefs, but determine that one bottom
line is racial (or economic, gender, ethnic, sexual orientation) inclusivity.
That is, excluding or being less than wholly (and, perhaps, holy) welcoming
to individuals of a particular group is simply unacceptable. That is the bottom line.

Or a church may acknowledge that varying understandings of Scripture are acceptable, as individuals are led by the Holy Spirit, but proclaim
that the congregation's bottom line is that Jesus is Lord.

Finally, Gifford proposes that we dream of how a church would look
that embodied and implemented answers to these questions. What would
the building look like, for example, if the congregation honored diverse physical
abilities? How would the congregation assembled for worship look if we
truly honored inclusivity in economic status, as well as race, ethnicity, and
sexual orientation? How would the monthly church calendar look if meetings, study groups, and other programs reflected our answers?

Undertaking such exercises involves hard spiritual and mental work,
but clearly it can produce a much clearer vision and one that inspires
commitment.

RESTATE THE VISION

How often do you read your church's mission statement? Do you remember what it says? Most often, it is tucked away in the by-laws and, once
approved, is never heard again. (And in some cases, churches have no
mission statement. I would encourage them to craft statements that reflect
their congregational identity.) One pastor told me that she prints her church's
mission statement in every weekly worship bulletin, and I suspect that other
churches have a similar practice. I attended one church where the pastor
preached a series of sermons on the mission statement, carefully examining
a phrase a week. Another congregation proclaims its mission on the sign in
the church's front yard. It is important that mission statements be frequently
articulated and widely shared in some way. Making at least the core sen-
tence of that statement a part of the church logo or standard bulletin and

newsletter masthead may be helpful. Reading it responsively or in unison at least once a year—perhaps at the beginning of an annual congregational meeting—is another technique.

REVISITING THE VISION

Some congregations intentionally and regularly review their mission statements, updating them when appropriate. At least once a year, they schedule an all-church retreat to brainstorm about where members and frequent attenders want their faith community to go, what they want it to be and to do. Three features of this exercise bear mentioning.

First, it is intentional. A specific time is set aside for this dialogue. It may involve a weekend retreat or simply a Saturday-morning brunch or Sunday-afternoon workshop.

Second, the effort aims at inclusivity. These retreats are not just for a few church leaders. Anyone who attends the church is encouraged to participate.

Third, these efforts are "regular"—scheduled every six months, every year, or every two years—to keep the members current with one another's interests, needs, and expectations. Without that regularity, a church might well discover that a mission statement framed when the congregation was founded is significantly out of step with current contexts and younger parishioners. That does not mean that the original statement has to be scrapped. But it probably needs regular, periodic fine-tuning to represent genuine consensus among current parishioners.

Shared, frequently stated, and periodically reviewed mission statements that have spiritual integrity and that recognize and value diversity and mutual respect can be important touchstones when conflict erupts. They should be highlighted at the beginning of a conflict-resolution process and repeated if the process seems to bog down, to remind parties of what they have agreed they hold in common.

Questions for Reflection

1. What are some of the expectations you and your fellow parishioners have of the church? Why do you and they attend your church? Can your church accommodate all of those expectations?

2. What is your church's identity? If new residents of your community asked about your church, how would you describe it? If they asked others in your community who are not members of your congregation to describe your church, what would the newcomers hear?

3. What images from Scripture most reflect your understanding of your congregation or the way you would like your congregation to be known?

4. What is your theological "bottom line"? What is your "central organizing principle"? What do you feel is essential for common agreement? What range of diverse views can you accommodate?

5. What is your congregation's mission statement? Does it accurately reflect who you are and what your faith community proclaims by its programs and the way it functions?

6. If it is not an accurate reflection of the congregation, how might it be rewritten? What process would you use to reformulate that statement?

Chapter 4

RESPONSIBILITY

AND

ACCOUNTABILITY

I'm staying out of trouble. I don't want to know what's going on. I just want to sit in my pew and do my job on the hospitality committee.

I'm not taking sides.

The minister [head deacon, ladies' guild secretary, choir director, head usher] told me what really happened. She wouldn't lie.

I really agree with Martin, but I don't want to make waves.

From what I hear, it's all David's fault. If he doesn't like it here, he ought to leave and find another church.

I just can't get involved. I have health problems and I have to avoid stressful situations. I haven't been sleeping well. I have all I can do to get through each day, and I just can't deal with anything more.

You can expect to hear all of the statements above, and more—more ways church members avoid being responsible and accountable—when conflict arises in congregations that are untrained and unprepared to deal with it in a healthy manner.

I have been involved for the past 25 years in United Church of Christ congregations, churches whose roots are "Congregational." That means that every member potentially has an equal say in determining policy. In many other Protestant denominations, members are similarly responsible for policy. Even in the more hierarchical bodies, members have some responsibilities for reaching informed conclusions and voicing them. Yet in too many congregations, many members sidestep those responsibilities and shy away from being accountable for their own behavior, especially when they are on the fringes of a conflict rather than at its center.

When many members not directly involved remove themselves from the dialogue, their absence can create a harmful vacuum. In the absence of a thoughtful, reasoning center that can encourage fair, responsible dialogue between or among opposing parties, those parties are likely to become more rigid than open in regard to resolving their dispute. In effect, using a boxing metaphor, they go to their respective corners and come out fighting. Parishioners who are not directly involved in the dispute but who do not walk away from the conversation can play significant roles that enhance opportunities for healthy resolution. Later, I will discuss some of those roles.

It may be helpful to examine some of those demurring statements at the beginning of this chapter as well as the motives behind them and the repercussions.

BYSTANDERS OR SPECTATORS?

I'm staying out of trouble. I don't want to know what's going on. I just want to sit in my pew and do my job on the hospitality committee.

Parishioners who voice these sentiments often are uncomfortable with conflict and will do just about anything to avoid it. They fear losing friends or becoming the target of criticism from those with whom they disagree. It just seems easier to remain silent and uninvolved.

In assigning roles to various parties in a conflict, Hugh Halverstadt, a veteran coach of parties in congregational disputes, distinguishes between "bystanders" and "spectators." Bystanders or "stockholders," as Halverstadt has more recently labeled those on the periphery of a dispute, "are more invested in how the principals resolve their differences than in what principals' resolutions may be." Bystanders may not be involved in the issue at hand, but they want a resolution that is a reconciling one. They are more interested in the resolution process than in the content of the dispute.[1] Passive spectators, on the other hand, contribute to the destructive nature of conflict. Some simply enjoy watching a fight, and others want to absent themselves until all the emotional blood and gore are mopped up.

In reality, few parishioners are likely to avoid being affected in some way by conflict in their congregation, no matter how much they might prefer to remain passive spectators. Halverstadt likens bystanders to parties in a fishing boat "in which principals get into a fight. Their primary concern is that the principals' behavior not sink the boat."[2] From my experience, they may even want to avoid getting splashed. The difference between appropriately engaged bystanders and disengaged spectators is this: Bystanders or stockholders understand that they have an interest in the way the fight is handled and that their participation in the process can steady the boat, while spectators fail to realize that they are likely to be splashed.

However, most people who have some role in the life of the church are likely to get splashed by conflict. A hospitality committee chair suddenly discovers that she has trouble securing greeters for Sunday worship because those directly involved in the conflict fear that they will either be shunned by those with whom they disagree or that they will make some members feel uncomfortable. The head usher similarly faces a dwindling pool of willing ushers. The chair of the annual church fair finds fewer volunteers to bake for the pie table. Adult youth-group leaders struggle to secure drivers for an outing. Those on the periphery ultimately have a stake in the conduct, if not the outcome, of a conflict. Those who accept the role of thoughtful bystanders also have responsibilities.

"A community of responsible bystanders can impose constraints on principals. These constraints may not resolve the issues but can prevent a win/lose resolution of the issues," Halverstadt points out.[3]

TAKING SIDES

I'm not taking sides.

That seemingly neutral statement may simply be a convenient way to mask a person's real agenda. Sometimes it just means, "I don't want to assume the responsibility I should take for becoming informed." For others, "I'm not taking sides" really means "I've already taken a side, and it's not yours, but I don't have the courage to tell you where I stand or to be accountable for having taken this side." And still others mouth this no-sides position when what they really should be acknowledging is "I'm playing both sides. I want to be on the winning side. Until I can figure out who is likely to win, I'll keep silent."

The person who truly is "not taking sides" might go on to say something like this: "I have spent some time trying to get at the facts and listening to people's feelings, and this is how I see it. The chair of the board of trustees has done [this], which hasn't been helpful. But the diaconate chair has done [that], which also has not been helpful. We need to sit down with these two people and maybe some others and talk this out. Maybe this is not even about 'sides.' Maybe this is about poor communication. We need to stop looking for someone to blame and explore how we can resolve this issue for the good of the congregation."

A fundamental problem in most church conflicts is viewing or framing problems in terms of sides when the issues often are far more complex. In her book *The Argument Culture: Moving from Debate to Dialogue*, Deborah Tannen, a Georgetown University linguistics professor whose books address communication clarity, observes:

> Our fondness for the fight scenario leads us to frame many complex human interactions as a battle between two sides. This then shapes the way we understand what happened and how we regard the participants. One unfortunate result is that fights make a mess in which everyone is muddied. The person attacked is often deemed just as guilty as the attacker.
>
> The argument culture limits the information we get rather than broadening it in another way. When a certain type of interaction is the norm, those who feel comfortable with that type of interaction are drawn to participate, and those who do not feel comfortable with it recoil and go elsewhere. If public discourse included a broad range of types, we would be making room for individuals with different temperaments to take part and contribute their perspectives and insights. But when debate, opposition, and fights overwhelmingly predominate, those who enjoy verbal sparring are likely to take part . . . and those who cannot comfortably take part in oppositional discourse or do not wish to, are likely to opt out.[4]

Spectators opt out. Bystanders can support and sometimes create the atmosphere in which folk of different temperaments, perspectives, and insights feel safe and are encouraged to engage in the discourse.

Tannen points out another destructive outcome of framing conflict in terms of sides. How often have you heard the adage, "Well, there are two sides to every story"? That assumes that no matter what positions are put forth, it is pretty much a draw. But in a section of her book subtitled "When Lies Become 'The Other Side,'" Tannen says, "[S]ometimes there is no other side; there is only one side: truth."[5]

In these cases, neutrality can take on an unmerited but supposedly admirable quality. Some people think that to *name* a problem involves improper *judging*. Yet there are situations in which we recognize that neutrality is an irresponsible response. The classic image of irresponsible neutrality is that of the "good Germans" who remained uninvolved in the face of the Holocaust. Many said they "didn't know" because they did not want to know. To *know* would require people of conscience to protest—indeed, to risk their lives. To *know* in a church conflict requires people of faith and conscience to risk discomfort.

Consider this hypothetical example of a situation in which there are not two sides:

> Bill McBride, a troubled, angry layperson, is so determined to force the pastor to leave that he is willing either to lie outright or to repeat grapevine gossip that subsequently proves untrue. "I hear that the pastor took $500 from the youth fellowship account to buy a pool table for his basement," McBride tells anyone who will listen, "and I'm sure he pocketed some deacons' fund money."

The two-sides adage would give McBride's unsubstantiated charges the same weight as the pastor's denial and reputation. But in this case, there is only one side: the truth. The pastor spent her own money for the pool table, and no inappropriate deacons' fund disbursements were made.

LIMITING OPTIONS

Framing hot-button issues in terms of "two sides" also prevents consideration of a wider range of options and new information, Tannen points out. In a section headed "'Two Sides' Gets in the Way of Solving Problems," she discusses how this approach limits fuller, more thoughtful examination of such issues as abortion, race, and drugs. For example, she says, reducing racial issues to a simple black-white dichotomy obscures the existence of many other races such as Asian, American Indian, Semitic, and Arab, and of people with biracial or multiracial backgrounds. When the drug issue is framed solely in terms of a battle between drug warriors and legalizers, Tannen explains, any proposal from one side is immediately discounted or demonized by the other. Similarly, viewing the abortion issue only in terms of hard-line pro-choice and pro-life factions is an obstacle to considering measures to reduce unwanted pregnancies that both groups might support.[6] When we insist that a congregational conflict be framed solely in terms of sides, winning becomes more important than searching for a healthy resolution.

Still another aspect of framing issues in terms of *sides* is that taking sides means, at least implicitly, accepting rules and behavioral expectations that severely limit the ability of individuals to process new information, adjust their perceptions, or look at the larger picture. Once you have "taken sides," total loyalty to that side is expected. These rules or expectations sometimes become explicit when they are violated. If you voice an observation that someone on the other side has a valid point, a friend may try to lay a guilt trip on you by saying, "Hey, I thought you were on *our* side." If you begin to perceive good points and bad points on both sides, you may well be labeled disloyal by those with whom you initially allied yourself. These same expectations of loyalty apply when new information might otherwise prompt you to reassess your position. Once sides are chosen, each becomes defensive and closed. Information from one perspective that sheds new light on the issue is routinely discarded by opponents without thoughtful examination. In fact, new information may be perceived as a threat to your side's solidarity. This liability of the "sides" framework holds true no matter which side you are on.

Consider congregational conflict that focuses on the pastor. One side is highly critical of the pastor because he has failed to visit longtime parishioners in the hospital, constantly changes elements of the worship service, and spends too much time in denominational and ecumenical activities outside the parish. The other side staunchly defends the minister because he has given them excellent pastoral care, preaches the kinds of sermons they want to hear, and seems to work really well with youth.

Enter some new information or perspectives. Joe, who has been on the critics' side, learns that no one bothered to tell the pastor that Mary and Jim had been hospitalized. "How could he visit them if he didn't know?" Joe asks his fellow critics. "Well, he should have known," they respond, essentially dismissing this new and relevant information. Carol, on the pastor-supporter side, has a conversation with a worship committee member who says, "Gee, I don't want to be critical, but the pastor never consults us about changes in the service." Hmmm, Carol ponders, and then says to fellow supporters of the pastor, "Maybe the pastor is ignoring an important piece of ministry-sharing between clergy and laity. That is a legitimate concern." "Hey," they respond, "he's the minister, and he should do what he wants." They dismiss this new observation.

These rules or expectations of both sides make life unpleasant for those who would try to bridge gaps and initiate some thoughtful and productive conversation to resolve conflict issues. One woman told me of her experience in this regard. She first staunchly supported her pastor, who was under attack. After he left, she came to understand that he had deeply wounded some parishioners. When she sought some of them out in an effort to be one instrument of congregational reconciliation, the clergy critics became angry, she said, because they felt she was letting them down.

> *The minister [head deacon, ladies' guild secretary, choir director, head usher] told me what really happened. She wouldn't lie.*

If you truly have good reason to trust any of these people, this may be a good starting point. If the person who told you "what really happened" is someone with a history of honesty and integrity, the information he or she shared may provide a sound benchmark against which to assess additional information. However, too often this statement means one of the following:

- "I really need to trust my minister. Reverend Sanborn has got to be telling the truth. I have put him on a pedestal, and I would be crushed if I thought he was lying."

- "I really need to trust my minister because I am facing serious surgery and need him," or "My wife just died and I need the comfort the minister provides."
- "The head deacon is one of my best customers, and I can't afford to lose his business."
- "The head usher is my son's history teacher, and I don't want to make things harder for Billy."
- "The ladies' guild secretary is my beautician."

In each case, the true believer may need to believe for fear of offending the party on whom he or she relies for pastoral care, business, a child's school fortunes, or a hairstyle.

I really agree with Martin, but I don't want to make waves.

Church conflicts seldom provide the luxury of pure neutrality, at least in effect. Following a fairly heated dispute involving denominational affiliation in one of my former congregations, a member said, "My wife and I really agreed with your views, but we didn't want to make waves." But they did make waves for me and others who favored one position because their actions had the effect of opposing that position. They made waves because we felt betrayed by people who privately expressed agreement with us but lacked the courage to say so publicly.

From what I hear, it's all David's fault. If he doesn't like it here, he ought to leave and find another church.

On rare occasions, this statement just might be true. If a woman whose theology is extremely, perhaps rigidly conservative, comes into a congregation with a clearly progressive vision, she probably should find a congregation whose theology is more consistent with her own. But too often, this statement is used to target a scapegoat or simply to seek elimination of those with whom we disagree. Elimination of those who speak up or ask uncomfortable questions is a key tactic when corporate denial is at work. Those who are outspoken or who ask questions often provide the first alerts of trouble. They are the messengers, and the message is: "We've got a problem." But congregations that want to deny that they have systemic problems are quick to edge out such folk by shunning or other unkind techniques. "Whew. Now that they're gone, everything will be fine," parishioners in these congregations are likely to say. They are often puzzled when the problems reappear later.

I just can't get involved. I have health problems and I have to avoid stressful situations. Since my husband died, I haven't been sleeping well. I have all I can do to get through each day, and I just can't deal with anything more.

Certainly there are folk who, because of personal circumstances, understandably think they must avoid any involvement in a stressful conflict and that we should respect their boundaries. However, I would urge them to reconsider for two reasons:

1. No matter how understandable one's explanation for opting out, if too many parishioners take this route, the vacuum remains and so does the resulting potential for destructive conflict rather than healthy dialogue and resolution.

2. If the result is destructive, the odds are that those opting out will not escape stress. Instead, the stress will just crop up in a different form. The man concerned about his blood pressure is likely to continue to feel tension whenever the congregation gathers—for worship, meetings, potluck suppers, whatever. The grieving widow may well find less support from her pastor and fellow parishioners because their energies are consumed by the conflict and its unhealthy aftermath.

Taking Responsibility

All of the above reflect *don'ts*. What should responsible church members *do*? Generally, parishioners can become informed and insist that the conflict-management process has integrity—that it is fair and respectful and thorough and that it is designed to achieve a win-win resolution that leaves no one with long-term wounds.

Responsible church members can:

1. Seek the best, most accurate sources of information and insist that these sources be made easily and readily available to all members, not just to a select few church leaders. Nothing is more harmful to the health of a congregation than uninformed or misinformed gossip. It is important to make

a distinction between gossip and appropriate information sharing. Congregations are communities, and in communities people talk informally with one another, as well they should. It is often through such informal conversation that we learn about each others' lives, experiences, joys, and hurts, appropriately sharing all of them in Christian love. If John is taken to the hospital with a critical injury in midweek, or if fire ravages the Millers' family home, this kind of informal communication can quickly mobilize church members into a support system of meals, child care, donated household goods, and prayerful concern. Gossip, on the other hand, is often full of misinformation, incomplete information, or even malicious lies. Once launched on a congregational grapevine, this kind of gossip can become toxic. It takes on a life of its own and is almost impossible to correct fully because the grapevine is so informal that there is no point of contact at which the misinformation can be completely and effectively corrected.

How do you obtain the best, most accurate sources of information? Regularly attend meetings—of the church council, the vestry, the session, the boards of deacons and trustees, the social action committee, or the religious education committee. Nothing beats hearing for yourself what is said, unfiltered by anyone else's perceptions. Even meeting minutes can be filtered by the often subconscious or unconscious feelings, emotions, or views of the recorder. For example, the social action committee chair announces a series of forums to provide "education" around issues of homosexuality. But the minutes, taken by a scribe uncomfortable with those issues, state that the forums will "indoctrinate" church members. Even less reliable is word of mouth. A diaconate decision to study the issue of inclusive language could become, as one hearer relates it, "changing the Lord's Prayer to begin with 'Our Mother, who art in heaven.' Can you believe that?" The mission committee's decision to give $100 to the local AIDS education program can become: "The mission committee is advocating the gay lifestyle."

Regular attendance at church committee and board meetings is important for several reasons. First, it provides parishioners with some continuing context. Items on the "old business" agenda may not be fully explained at subsequent meetings. Further, bystanders can hold boards and committees responsible if these witnesses have followed an issue through several sessions. If something is said at one session that conflicts with statements made at an earlier session, bystanders can point out the contradiction and request clarification. They can also generally provide an element of ongoing accountability for board and committee deliberations and actions simply by their interested and informed presence. Elected church officers will be less prone to take potentially harmful shortcuts or make irresponsible remarks if parishioners are present as witnesses. I suspect that boards and committees are more likely to adhere to consistently healthy processes when they have regular audiences.

Second, regular attendance avoids sudden surges in audience numbers when critical issues arise—a surge that tends to heighten everybody's anxiety. "I always know something is up when suddenly a lot of people show up for a meeting," one pastor told me. Still, when critical issues do arise, it is even more important that parishioners have firsthand knowledge of how they are handled. Critical issues are most likely to spawn abundant congregational conversation. In healthy congregations, that conversation is well informed.

Some churches, by policy or tradition, may not be accustomed to welcoming visitors to committee and board meetings. Lay leaders might consider changing these policies and practices to encourage visitor attendance unless issues requiring confidentiality are on the agenda.

Of course, not every church member can attend every committee or board meeting. Meeting minutes are the next-best source, since any significant errors in the first drafts are likely to be corrected by cooler, more objective heads at the next meeting. Minutes of the meetings should be readily available, preferably posted in an easily accessible location or, even better, reproduced in the monthly church newsletter. If meeting minutes are kept in the church office, members should be encouraged to seek photocopies so they can reread them. Members who are able should offer to pay minimal fees to cover photocopying costs. Making meeting minutes easily available to members seems so evident that stating it may seem superfluous. Yet in one church, a member who regularly asked to see minutes of various board meetings was officially chastised for being nosy. Somehow, an assumption had evolved that anyone who asked to see that information must be a troublemaker or, at least, did not trust the pastor or elected church leaders. Word of that criticism quickly spread and had a chilling effect. Other parishioners concluded that it was not safe to ask for meeting minutes, so they began to rely on hearsay.

2. Participate thoughtfully in discussions about policies and processes, support elected leaders who uphold and implement them, and hold accountable those who do neither. Staying relatively faithful to such policies and

processes is not, as some may suggest, stuffy legalism. Instead, it ensures consistency and fair play and provides mechanisms to deal with small problems before they become big ones. When processes are inconsistent and policies are sometimes observed and sometimes ignored, the result will be insecurity and chaos. If everyone is relatively sure that sound policies and practices are in place and in operation, they know what to expect. They can relate to others with a feeling of comfort and safety. If sound policies and procedures are not in place or are abused or ignored, depending on the whims of the pastor or some lay leaders, members do not know what to expect and may shrink from participation.

Let me suggest some scenarios in which policies are either unclear, inconsistently applied by leaders, or inconsistently supported by parishioners. Each is a recipe for conflict with little likelihood of healthy resolution.

a. If there is no clearing house for complaints about the pastor, these complaints are voiced through the grapevine, often getting embellished in the process, and the pastor has no way to address them—either to make desired changes or to defend the action discussed. The same holds true if no stated process exists for handling complaints about lay leaders. With no established procedure to deal with such complaints, the pastor or layperson may be unfairly maligned or have no opportunity to amend his or her ways. Without an established procedure, those who have concerns become increasingly frustrated, thinking they are not being heard. At the same time, the targets of the grapevine complaints grow increasingly uneasy, because they are aware of dissension but unable to address it.

b. A church's by-laws stipulate that decisions committing a congregation to spend more than $1,000 outside the regular budget must be made by the members, but trustees decide they should sign the $10,000 contract with an investment consultant. After all, trustees reason, a lot of parishioners just would not understand esoteric financial issues. Parishioners may feel betrayed and demeaned by such an action.

c. The pastor's contract says the pastor shall function "in consultation with and with the advice of the deacons." The pastor decides to make major changes in the worship service, initiate a controversial evening study series, or simply strike a half-dozen people from his pastoral calling list without consulting the deacons. The deacons find themselves at an impasse with the pastor and reluctantly take the issue to the congregation. If parishioners then say, in essence, "Oh, back off—

forget the contract; let the pastor do whatever he likes," the deacons are left in limbo. Few laypeople will want to accept church offices if they are not sure when and if the congregation expects them to enforce or implement stated policies. If the ultimate decisions on these matters are left to the whim of the moment or to the strongest personalities, congregational officers may fear they are in constant jeopardy of making a move that the congregation will not support.

3. Insist on accountability. Each person should be accountable for what he or she says and does.

a. Ultimately, the pastor is accountable either to the congregation (in a church with congregational polity), or to a bishop or district superintendent. But in every church, there should be clearly written and understood policies and practices defining to whom or to what board the pastor is accountable for day-to-day functioning. This seems self-evident and yet, in too many churches, this issue remains blurry. And when it is blurry, it is an area ripe for conflict. If some parishioners are unhappy with some element of the worship service, to whom should they turn? If they want the pastor to do more home visitation, whom do they tell? Without a clear policy and practice of accountability, too often they simply talk to each other, and neither the pastor nor the relevant lay leaders hear the complaints about the needs firsthand and early. That is a recipe for trouble. The complaints simply circulate and often get embellished along the grapevine. By the time they are finally aired in any formal way, a meeting has been called to fire the pastor or to recall certain lay leaders. At other times, complaints just continue to simmer, with disgruntled parishioners quietly cutting back on their financial pledges and volunteer efforts. At this point, it will take much more time and effort to unravel what is really causing the unrest.

b. Similarly, parishioners should be held accountable. The best way we can hold each other accountable is to avoid participating in "triangulation"—the increasingly popular buzz word for simply talking about a person rather than to him or her. It is Ken talking to Brenda about a problem Ken has with Bruce. At best, even if the information is communicated correctly, the person being talked about feels frustrated, if not betrayed. That person cannot respond if he or she is not directly confronted. At worst, triangulating can turn into backstabbing. When people can avoid being held accountable for what they say, some may be tempted to stretch the truth, exaggerate it, or simply lie. Bystander

Brenda can encourage healthy behavior by saying to Ken, "I really think you should talk this over directly with Bruce. That's the only way you two are going to straighten this out." In a healthy congregation, bystanders refuse to be drawn into such triangles. When Dick says to Martin, "You can tell the pastor that some people are really upset with her sermon on Sunday," Martin should reply, "Dick, you need to tell the pastor yourself. And be careful about using that term 'some people.' Speak for yourself and encourage others who are upset to do the same."

c.   Healthy congregations refuse to deal with anonymous complaints or allegations, whether they are directed at clergy or parishioners. Of course, the most insidious form of this practice is the unsigned letter. But it is also important to resist listening to, without clarification, statements such as "A lot of people were upset with that sermon," or "Some people think the Sunday school curriculum is inadequate." Those who make such statements should be asked to name or at least number the complainants. Is "a lot" five or 50? Is "some" a dozen or only my best friend and I?

4. Urge the pastor, committees, and boards to seek candid feedback actively and regularly. Those with questions and even with complaints need to be treated with respect and not targeted for abuse because they raise issues that make some parishioners uncomfortable.

5. Insist on fair play or, as Halverstadt puts it in the case of a conflict-management process, "fair fighting." Bystanders may not be heavily invested in the substance of a dispute or even in its ultimate resolution, but they can influence the conduct of the resolution process. Further, they can be wounded if that process is unfair.

What are some ways bystanders can support fair fighting?

- They can monitor the discussion and insist that it be mutually respectful, avoid name-calling, and remain focused.
- When tempers flare, they can call a time-out.
- They can serve as "coaches" to help parties hone fair fighting skills and better articulate their positions, as Halverstadt suggests.
- They can continue to lift up process issues and the need for win-win resolutions that will benefit the entire congregation. Bystanders can intervene when disputes get to the either/or stage and ask for suggestions of additional options. After listening to the discussion, bystanders may even come up with some new suggestions.

When members develop good habits of responsibility and accountability, the problems and minor conflicts that are inevitable in any congregation can be handled in a healthy manner. In a fit congregation, responsible members will understand that when a dispute arises, they have a stake in the resolution process and should seek the best information possible, speak directly to those with whom they differ, and expect to be held accountable for what they say and do.

Questions for Reflection

1. How have members not directly involved in congregational disputes functioned in your church—as active bystanders or passive spectators? What keeps the spectators from accepting responsible bystander roles?

2. Have you, as a spectator or bystander, ever been "splashed" or "dunked" by a conflict in your congregation? How? How did you feel?

3. How do you acquire information about the actions and discussions of church boards and committees? Do you think you have free access to appropriate information? If not, what are the obstacles to such access?

4. How are your church by-laws and other stated processes followed or not followed? Discuss situations in which they were followed and times when they were not. Were the outcomes different and, if so, how?

5. What opportunities do parishioners have to provide feedback to the pastor, committees, and boards? How might this process be improved?

6. To whom is the pastor accountable? To whom are boards and committees accountable?

7. Do you have a clear process for handling complaints against or concerns about the pastor, lay leaders, boards, and committees? How might it be improved?

Chapter 5

REDUCING ANXIETY

No matter what we do, another person leaves the church. I'm afraid to propose anything.

I don't get much out of worship these days. I never know who's speaking to whom. And I'm afraid to talk about much more than the weather at the coffee hour.

I don't dare ask any more questions about the finances. The last time I did, those people just glared at me.

That's it. I've had it. I'm out of here.

Everything was fine until that new board of deacons took office. Let's call a congregational meeting and get rid of them.

At first glance, about the only thing these comments seem to have in common is that they signal trouble. That is certainly true. But there is another commonality among them—high anxiety. It plays out in different ways, but the result is the same: stalemate or escalation. Fit congregations seek win-win solutions, but anxiety pushes us to win-lose or even lose-lose outcomes.

The most pervasive message from workshops and books on conflict management in the church is that the manager must remain a *nonanxious presence*, no matter how stressful the situation and no matter how elements trigger his or her personal reactions. That lesson has been especially hard for me to learn and then practice. When I view some behavior that seems wrong to me, I want to attack it with a strong dose of self-righteous indignation. And I have a similarly strong compulsion to try to "fix" things. Neither inclination is very helpful. The only thing I can "fix" is me. And when I am bent on "fixing" the behavior of others, I am anxious.

Even the most serene conflict manager will face a difficult, if not impossible, task if the parties to the conflict are anxiously reactive. When we are "anxiously reactive," we *react* out of our anxiety. Instead, we need to *respond* out of thoughtfulness. It follows, then, that a congregation in training to handle inevitable conflict within its life and to enjoy growth from resolving that conflict must develop lay leaders who understand and can practice the art of nonanxious presence. What skills are necessary?

LISTEN THOUGHTFULLY

I struggle with this discipline, and I suspect that I am not alone. As soon as a conversation becomes energized—let alone adversarial—and its subject holds some importance for me, I tend to shut out or only half-hear what others are saying. I am too busy planning what I will say as soon as the others finish. In that mode, I become overanxious—to make my case, to defend myself, or to declare others wrong. I have found that thoughtful listening reduces my anxiety. It prompts me to step back a bit from my emotional investment in the conversation.

A variety of available resources are devoted to helping us develop so-called active listening skills. Most point to this common failing—that we are so busy preparing to make our own points in an argument that we simply do not hear what others are saying. As a result, the "others" sense that they have not been respected by being truly heard. Further, we often either totally miss their message or misread it. Those powerful results fuel anxiety and frustration and, consequently, ratchet conflict up a notch or two.

Consider how poor listening skills feed anxiety:

1. If, after I have spoken, I think that no one has really heard what I said, I feel disrespected—put down. The normal reaction is to assume that no one cares how I feel or what I have to say. My next reaction: Why bother? I give up. My feelings or observations or experiences just do not count here. And in that mood, I am even less likely to listen to the one who has failed to listen to me. My anxiety is ratcheted up a notch.

2. If I am so busy preparing my own statement that I hear nothing of what others are saying, I may miss important clues that point to some possible common ground. Witness how this failure to hear plays out in an example of a conflict over passing the peace:

JOE: We're a pretty traditional congregation. Most of us dislike all this jumping up, walking the aisles, and hugging folks. This disrupts the worship atmosphere. And Sunday worship is very important to me. I wonder why these people come to church at all. Those who think this is such a hot idea ought to go down the road to that Holy Roller church.
RUTH: Passing the peace is one of the most important parts of worship for me. It makes folks feel welcome and loved. It really made me feel at home the first time I came here. We talk about bringing in new members, but I wonder if some people would just as soon keep this church for themselves. If we don't reach out and show people they are welcome, they are not going to stay.

If Ruth had really listened to Joe, she would have heard, among the angry words, "[W]orship is very important to me." After all, Ruth also affirmed the importance of worship. How might this dialogue have turned out differently?

RUTH: Joe, I can see what you're getting at. This is something new for many of the longtime members, and it probably feels strange to them. Worship is very important to all of us. But there are others of us who really find passing the peace meaningful. Let's think about some ways we might be able to do it that might feel less disruptive. Maybe we can, for the most part, just greet those near us and stay in our pews. But we need to be sure visitors and new folks are greeted. Let's talk about it at the next church council meeting.

That kind of response might significantly ratchet down the anxiety level of the debate.

3. If I am so bent on my own agenda that I mishear what others say, I am likely to take offense where none was meant and then respond inappropriately. Instead of hearing some commonality or even hearing strong opposition to passing the peace, Ruth responds, "Well, since those of us who want to continue passing the peace might as well not come to church at all and aren't very good Christians, maybe we will just leave." But Joe did not

say those with whom he has a difference of opinion are not good Christians. One way to practice thoughtful listening is to echo what you believe you have heard. That is, when Joe makes a statement, Ruth must, before replying with her own statement, restate what Joe said to Joe's satisfaction. If she had done this, the dialogue might have played out this way:

> RUTH: I hear you saying that those of us who want to continue passing the peace aren't good Christians.
> JOE: Whoa. I never said that.
> RUTH: But you said you wondered why we came to church at all. And you suggested we leave and go to another church that you put down.
> JOE: Yeah, but that's not the same as saying you're not good Christians. Actually, I kind of got carried away there. Of course, I don't want people to leave the church. But that's what I heard you threatening.
> RUTH: No, that wasn't a threat. At least I didn't mean it to be, although I admit it might have sounded like one. What I do mean is that it's important to share God's love by personally connecting with newcomers. If we don't, they might move on to another church.

A couple of things happened in that last exchange. Joe both clarified what he said and acknowledged that he "got carried away," while Ruth, too, was able to clarify her view. Equally important, the tone of the exchange mellowed a bit. By the end of this piece of conversation, both Joe and Ruth sound a little less anxious and a little more open to finding some common ground.

Thoughtful listening can lead us to engage in dialogue rather than argument or debate. Joseph Phelps, Baptist minister and workshop leader, devotes an entire book to this subject: *More Light, Less Heat: How Dialogue Can Transform Christian Conflicts into Growth*. It is an extremely valuable resource, and I urge lay leaders who seek to advance their congregation's fitness to exercise the disciplines he recommends. Dialogue is especially critical for faith communities, Phelps maintains, because

> in dialogue, we open ourselves up to God, to a wisdom from Above that transcends the dialogue and sheds new light on our corporate discord and darkness. To enter into dialogue is to accept the possibility that God could choose to reveal truth through our adversary, or through new self-discovery as we reveal ourselves before the other, or through the interchange of convictions.[1]

LIVE WITH AMBIGUITY

We tend to feel most secure and least anxious when situations are clear and forthright, when answers to questions or problems are obvious and absolute. When my gas gauge hovers near empty, a clear, simple solution is at hand—stop at the next service station and fill up the tank. When the church sanctuary feels chilly, the solution is obvious—turn up the thermostat.

But neither the Scriptures nor many of the situations we encounter as congregations provide that degree of clarity. At one point, Christ tells his disciples, "Peace I leave with you; my peace I give to you" (John 14: 27a). But in another gospel, Christ warns, "Do not think that I have come to bring peace to the earth; I have not come to bring peace, but a sword" (Matthew 10:34). One of the Ten Commandments urges us to honor our father and mother, but Jesus shocks us by saying, "For I have come to set a man against his father, and a daughter against her mother" (Matthew 10:35). We are called to seek justice and, at the same time, to turn the other cheek. What are we to make of these seemingly stark contradictions? An interim pastor of my church suggested that the Bible is full of these paradoxes. A "paradox," according to my dictionary, may be "a statement or proposition seemingly self-contradictory, but in reality expressing a possible truth." I like to think that we study Scripture to seek that possible truth.

Psychiatrist M. Scott Peck, who has written widely on spiritual development, makes a similar point:

> Most people dislike thinking about paradox and will attempt to flee from its inherent tension by running with just one side or another. But the spiritual journey is the quest for the whole truth, and the path of spiritual progress lies in embracing paradox.[2]

We face this kind of dilemma when one segment of the congregation seeks or even demands more contemporary music and inclusive language in prayers and hymns, while another digs in its heels and insists on traditional music and prayer, and unaltered hymn texts. We are similarly torn when a minister provides the best pastoral care a congregation has ever experienced but turns out to be a mediocre preacher. Too often in situations such as these, our longing for safety in simple answers kicks in, and we respond to the "herd instinct." Uncomfortable with ambiguity, we crowd together with others who insist on their simple answer, which in turn causes problems for others. We may even feel ambivalent about contemporary versus traditional music or about inclusive language. But ambivalence or ambiguity feels scary, so we enlist in one of the "sides" to feel safe.

Whenever I encounter ambiguity in Scripture or congregational problems, I am drawn to the powerful advice of poet Rainer Maria Rilke. In one of his *Letters to a Young Poet*, Rilke counsels the reader "to have patience with everything unresolved in your heart and to try to love the questions themselves as if they were locked rooms or books written in a very foreign language. Don't search for the answers. . . . Live the questions now."[3]

Living with ambiguity means *loving and living the questions* rather than desperately seeking answers. I find that image of loving a question helpful and healing. If I love the question, I can gently turn it over in my mind, explore its many facets and find a place of serene expectation. We live and love the questions when we engage in prayerful Bible study, staying open to God's voice and direction. Living and loving biblical paradoxes may mean tuning in to each piece—both justice-seeking and turn-the-other-cheek humility—and remaining open to God's guidance in specific situations.

Similarly, to live with the question of whether or not to employ inclusive language in liturgy and hymn singing may simply involve recognizing and respecting the feelings of people on both sides of the issue and patiently awaiting a time when those people might develop similar respect for each other's feelings. Living the question of how to evaluate a minister with exceptional pastoral counseling abilities and mediocre preaching gifts may be to do just that—live with the situation and be open to God at work in the pastor and the congregation.

Whatever the issue, insisting on answers to complicated questions tends to heighten anxiety. Living and loving the questions eases anxiety. I do not have to find the correct answer this minute or this day or this week. I can live with the ambiguity, trusting that God will reveal, in God's time, the faithful answer. That seems to be what Paul was getting at when he advised:

> Do not worry about anything, but in everything by prayer and supplication with thanksgiving let your requests be made known to God. And the peace of God, which surpasses all understanding, will guard your hearts and minds in Christ Jesus. (Philippians 4:6-7)

SEEK FEEDBACK

When we gang up with one side or the other to suppress our anxiety, we usually close ourselves off from new information and new perspectives. Part of living with ambiguity, of living and loving a thorny question, is pondering new information and new perspectives. That is why it is helpful and healthful to intentionally seek the viewpoints of others. I would suggest two categories of "others."

1. *Wise elders.* Among parishioners in most congregations are one or more longtime members who know a great deal about the church's history and its people, care deeply about its future, and have developed a kind of mellow outlook that takes a broader view rather than one limited to a narrow personal agenda. That caveat is important. Some elders can become stuck, perhaps understandably, in a particular place and totally resist any change. However, other older members not so heavily invested in a particular position can provide important background, context, and perspective. In my own case, I came to consult frequently one older woman in my congregation to get a sense of how the congregation or segments of it might react to various proposals or actions.

2. *Those with whom you disagree.* In an atmosphere of calm conversation, you can sometimes learn a great deal from someone "on the other side of the fence." Calm conversation, that dialogue Phelps describes, provides an opportunity for less emotionally charged exchanges than is often available in committee, board, or congregational meetings. Again, you may discover some points of commonality. Or you may come to understand better why this person holds an opposing view, how it might arise out of a set of earlier experiences. You may hear ideas that had never occurred to you before. At the very least, you can create and nurture a climate that may be more mutually respectful and less antagonistic. Again, in the midst of a conflict in my congregation, I purposely sought out a man with whom I had fundamental disagreements. In the process, we did discover some common ground. Further, when it became clear that we strongly disagreed on some points, we were able to reach a more comfortable understanding—to agree to disagree without fighting.

Seeking feedback is like opening a window in a stale room. It lets in the fresh air of fresh ideas.

KEEP A BALANCED LIFE AND OUTLOOK

When we are in the midst of a church conflict, chances are that we are heavily invested in the life of our congregation. It is precisely because we care so much that we are in the middle of the problem. If we did not care a great deal, we would be among the bystanders and spectators. In these situations, we tend to put all or almost all of our emotional eggs in the church basket. To strain that metaphor, when the church is in conflict, the basket gets shaken and we fear our emotional eggs will crack or be broken. And that makes us anxious. We can reduce that anxiety by placing some of our personal eggs in other baskets—family, hobbies, sports.

Another hard lesson for me was this need to be intentional about spending some leisure time doing things totally unrelated to the life of my congregation. Maintaining a balanced life—a balance among family, job, volunteer activities, and just plain fun—is always important and especially so when congregational conflict adds to our normal load of stress. We are much more likely to maintain an inner calm and a nonanxious presence in the life of the church when we take time to read a good novel; go to a movie; play golf, tennis, or pickup basketball; work on a hobby—anything that provides pleasure and an opportunity to unwind. Then we can return to the congregational arena refreshed and, again, with a more balanced personal perspective.

LAUGH A BIT

Finally, a healthy sense of humor is a key ingredient in developing a nonanxious presence. In the middle of a church mess (for that is often what a congregational conflict seems to be), we can become perpetually grim, if not depressed. That is when we need to find some space to lighten up. Since I became computer literate, my e-mail correspondents keep me supplied with lots of occasions for laughter as they forward the best funny stories they have encountered. When I begin to feel too wrapped up in a problem, I head for the comedy aisle at my local video rental store. Sometimes we can find humorous irony in the midst of the church problem, so long as our humor is not hurtful to others. The most liberating humor, I have discovered, grows out of my ability to laugh at myself. It periodically delivers me from my own tendency to self-righteousness. When I can chuckle at my own flaws, I am more relaxed and less anxious.

To develop and maintain a nonanxious presence: listen well; live and love the tough questions, and let the answers come in God's time; seek out the views of others; balance your church involvement with unrelated leisure pursuits; and laugh—at yourself, when possible. Emotionally fit parishioners contribute mightily to congregational fitness.

Questions for Reflection

1. When you are feeling anxious, how do you react to other people? How are your reactions different when you are feeling little or no anxiety?

2. Have there been times when you have not listened well to others? How did that feel? Did you miss anything or misunderstand what was being said? Practice some reflective listening, echoing the statements of others until they are satisfied that you really heard what they said.

3. How might it feel to "live and love" a tough question rather than push for an immediate answer? How do you feel physically when you are told that you don't have to answer a particularly tough question immediately, that you have time to ponder it? Can you notice muscle tension easing?

4. Who might provide healthy feedback to you about issues in your congregation?

5. Can you recall times when laughter relieved your anxiety? How did that feel, and how did it alter your approach to the problem at hand?

Chapter 6

REPEAL THE NO-TALK RULE

I'm really angry. I hear the trustees voted to spend $10,000 to redo the kitchen when the nursery is in tatters and half the kids' Sunday school chairs are broken.

Just let it go. We don't want to stir up any trouble.

The church council called two executive sessions last month. I hear they really beat up on the mission committee for putting up those AIDS posters. I think the mission committee was right. If there's a disagreement, let's get it out in the open so we have a chance to voice our opinions.

We don't need any more conflict. Everything's been so peaceful in worship. Let well enough alone.

All of a sudden the minister has us chanting this New Age stuff in worship. If I didn't think people would be upset with me, I'd go to a deacons' meeting to find out what's going on, but I don't want to get blamed for starting something.

Each of these comments cited reflects unease, anxiety, and frustration. Those are familiar simmering emotions among parishioners in a congregation that lives by the "no-talk" rule. Of course, it is an unwritten rule, but it is consistently enforced. Violators are quickly labeled "troublemakers," and it does not take long for others to get the message: Raising uncomfortable issues is unacceptable in this church.

The no-talk rule is based on several assumptions.

1. If we do not talk about it, it will go away.
2. If we do not talk about it, we can keep the peace.
3. If we do not talk about it, we will not upset anyone.

All of those assumptions are wrong. *It* will not go away. Whatever it is may seem to fade for a while, but in its dormant stage it will probably fester. The issue may seem to disappear, but the anger and frustration nourished by refusing to talk about it will almost certainly surface again somewhere—maybe a year or two later around another issue. When those emotions do surface, chances are that they will be even more intense than the feelings evoked by the original issue or problem.

In their book *Church Fights: Managing Conflict in the Local Church*, Speed Leas and Paul Kittlaus, church conflict authorities, warn:

> Where groups tend to suppress conflict, there will be an accumu-
> lation of feeling, leading toward a potentially dangerous conflict. A
> group in conflict can be like a pressure cooker: as the heat (con-
> flict) increases, the pressure builds up. The more pressure, the
> greater the explosion if the pressure is not abated. Without con-
> tinuous releases as a church moves along through its routine and
> small conflicts, pressure can build up causing a large explosion
> over a rather minor conflict.[1]

Whatever peace is achieved by not talking about an issue is superfi-
cial—more temporary truce than genuine peace. It will not even feel truly peaceful, because refusing to bring the issue to light will continue or exacer-
bate an undercurrent of unease. Most of us have been in situations—per-
haps in an extended family or a social group, if not our church—in which everyone knows there is a problem, but talking about it is considered unac-
ceptable. We refer to our behavior as "walking on eggshells," or "threading our way through a minefield" or "tiptoeing around" the subject. However that behavior is described, it produces stress. Anyone who has experienced such continued stress knows that it feels anything but peaceful.

Some time ago, following several years of tension in my church, we still had not examined, as a congregation, what had happened. A fellow parishioner at first resisted having any more conversation about the issues, in-
sisting that we needed to put the whole thing behind us. But then she added,

"From now on I'm just going to be a pew-sitter. I'm not taking any office." I gently suggested that her sentiments indicated that she had not put the issue behind her and that she still felt this undercurrent of unease. "You're right," she agreed. "I didn't think about it that way." Referring to the assumption that silence will ensure peace, Kenneth Halstead, Lutheran minister and family therapist, observes in his book *From Stuck to Unstuck: Overcoming Congregational Impasse*, "Congregations that do not know how to affirm and hear anger, how to set up 'safe' rules and structures of conflict and to make sure everyone fights fair, have relationships stuck in superficiality."[2]

Further, compelling silence about a problem will upset those who are affected by the problem. They may conclude that no one really cares about them or about how they feel. If the problem and the impact are ongoing, they may understandably feel like victims with no recourse, and eventually they may leave the church.

A MISNOMER

The "no-talk" rule is really misnamed. More accurately, it is a no-talk-in-official-circles rule. It means that talking about uncomfortable issues or problems at church council, vestry, session, deacons, trustees, or congregational meetings is taboo. Instead, the "talk" is on the unofficial fringes—on the phone, in the parking lot, in the supermarket aisle, or in private coffee klatches. In fact, the so-called no-talk rule usually increases this kind of informal, unofficial talk. Whenever parishioners are feeling unease, anxiety, and frustration, they are going to talk—but only to those within their small circles with whom they feel safe. And it is likely that the talk will become increasingly exaggerated and inaccurate. But because talk at official meetings is discouraged, there is no arena where exaggerations, misinterpretations, misunderstandings, or flat-out lies can be corrected, and there is no means to communicate the corrections to the congregation. Too often, the no-talk rule not only fails to ensure peace but also makes the initial problem worse. By the time the fringe talk has circulated in those telephone, parking-lot, or store-aisle conversations, the initial problem likely has become much more complicated and serious.

Consider the conversation cited at the beginning of this chapter about an alleged trustee decision to spend money on kitchen renovation rather than on Sunday school equipment. By the time the fringe talk has made the rounds, the message may be that the trustees' vote was a protest against the current Sunday school curriculum, an action to put the pastor in her place, or the result of a feud between a trustee and a teacher; that the women's guild blackmailed trustees by refusing to host congregational dinners without an updated kitchen; that a major contributor threatened to withhold his pledge unless the kitchen was redone. Sunday school teachers may consider resigning—quietly, of course, since official talk about the problem is discouraged. Before long, the entire congregation may be involved in one way or another—angry or confused, but with no way to express those feelings openly or to discover the truth. The initial problem has mushroomed.

Perhaps the most significant victim of the no-talk rule is a sense of congregational safety and trust. What does it mean for a church to be a safe place? As noted earlier, it is within our community of faith that our deepest feelings are touched. It is there that we not only pour out our cares, worries, pains, and joys to God in prayer, but hope to share a good bit of who we are with others in Christian fellowship. When the no-talk rule and its accompanying denial and avoidance behavior take hold, we begin to withhold pieces of ourselves from that congregational fellowship. We fear asking questions—about a mission project, the budget, or a deeply felt theological concern—lest our questions be met with silence, unfriendly stares, glares, or even criticism.

Sooner or later the resulting unease interferes with our ability to be spiritually nourished in worship. Several parishioners in one congregation said they were so anxious about the church's survival that they were distracted and seldom were able to focus on prayer or hear much of the sermon. In another, several members spent most of the worship time checking out or thinking about who was speaking to whom.

SPARE THE MESSENGERS

We have all heard the adage about what happens to the bearer of bad news. We may even have seen or experienced something like that. Doctors who have to tell patients or their families about a serious or terminal illness may find relatives' fear-borne anger directed back at them. Blaming the bearer of bad news is especially tempting when we are in denial—when we sense that the message is true but we do not want to deal with it.

The folk most likely to be wounded in no-talk congregations are the occasional few who know there are problems and possess enough self-confidence to speak about them and seek solutions. Sometimes these messengers already have been victimized in one way or another by whatever dysfunctional behavior is going on in the church. "[Victims] are often revictimized by the congregation when they try to tell the truth. They are not believed. They are the recipients of anger because they have caused disruption," warns Mark Laaser, a consultant on sexual addiction, in *Restoring the Soul of a Church: Healing Congregations Wounded by Clergy Sexual Misconduct*, which he co-edited. Although that book specifically addresses issues of congregational wounding by clergy sexual misconduct, the principle which Laaser articulates applies to many other types of congregational conflict.[3]

Parishioners who inquire about a series of discrepancies in a church treasurer's report may be chronic nitpickers. Or they may be sounding an alarm that the church is headed for serious financial problems or a case of financial misconduct. Parishioners who say they have witnessed repeated angry outbursts on the part of a committee chair or the pastor may be overreacting or pursuing a personal vendetta. Or they may be sounding an alarm that the chair or pastor has some serious emotional problems that are destructive to the congregation's health. Parishioners who allege that too many changes have been injected into the order of worship may be inflexible and cranky. Or they may be sounding an alarm of growing, legitimate congregational discontent with the pastor or lay leaders who make arbitrary decisions without adequately preparing parishioners for change.

It is not easy to discern the important difference between the nitpickers, overreactors, and inflexible cranks, on the one hand, and those voicing legitimate, responsible concerns. In a no-talk congregation, it is even more difficult. Accurate discernment will be much more likely in congregations that encourage questions and responses rather than stifling them.

REJECT DENIAL

Messengers are more likely to be scapegoated for the problems they uncover in congregations that observe the no-talk rule—a rule that, in turn, nourishes denial. Congregations that have been badly wounded by previous conflict that they failed to handle appropriately are much more likely to deny the dangers of the next conflict. Parishioners may feel that they are emotionally drained and simply cannot handle another conflicted situation, so they devote a good bit of energy to denying that there is one. That is the first cost of denial—energy. It takes an enormous amount of energy to deny the increasingly obvious, to make excuses, to stifle others and sometimes to guard and protect one or more badly behaving lay leaders, parishioners, or even the pastor.

In his book *The Pastor's Survival Manual: 10 Perils in Parish Ministry and How to Handle Them,* Presbyterian minister Kenneth Alan Moe, a pastor to pastors, lays out a typical scenario involving denial of a pastor's problem. It could apply as well to problems with lay leaders or other parishioners. Referring to the religious authority usually granted a pastor, Moe says:

> Respect for the office prevents some people from complaining until the pastor's behavior becomes openly outrageous. Even then a few folks would rather be quiet and pray for miraculous improvement than address the problem behavior. And codependent board members protect their pastor from the wrath of any who would complain. . . . The human buffer zone can provide protection, sometimes for years, but eventually, a few credible complaints about the pastor's behavior will creep out around the edges. Once the protective wall has been breached, increasing numbers of angry parishioners will besiege the pastor in denial.[4]

Such denial mechanisms can function, as well, to overprotect committees, choir directors, or even a well-organized, if informal, collection of antagonistic parishioners from being held accountable for their behavior. Sometimes, that buffer is simply collective congregational silence. Sometimes it takes the form of a kind of palace guard—around the pastor, an abusive lay leader, or a loose-cannon committee or board. Whatever the form of congregational denial—silence or a palace guard—the problem does not disappear. Instead, as Moe points out, eventually it will surface as a crisis—too serious to be ignored and often much more serious than the original problem.

DISTINGUISH CONFIDENTIALITY FROM SECRECY

Repealing the no-talk rule does not mean that anything is fair game for conversation. Some subjects require confidentiality. Both confidentiality and secrecy involve issues of trust and potential betrayal. When comments and concerns that appropriately should be kept confidential are broadcast, trust is betrayed. At the same time, trust is also betrayed when information parishioners should know is kept secret.

Clearly every congregation has situations that require pastors and sometimes lay leaders to keep confidences. Any pastoral counseling session is one of those situations. People who seek clergy counsel about personal problems should be assured that what they say will remain confidential. They will feel painfully betrayed if the pastor discusses their problems with other parishioners. The same ethical code applies to lay leaders who may be approached by church members seeking advice about personal issues and who similarly must keep such contacts and concerns confidential. As a deacon, I was privileged to have several parishioners in my church share some painful episodes in their lives. Mostly, I suspect, they just needed a caring listener, and I tried to be that for them. Still, I was deeply moved by their trust in me. Mission committees or other bodies that allocate funds to needy people also should maintain confidentiality about recipients and their situations, although the amounts expended should be reported to the congregation, perhaps with some general explanations that protect recipients' anonymity.

Secrets, on the other hand, can be incredibly destructive to congregational health. The most common types of secrets involve the concept of triangulation: Alice has a bone to pick with Carol, but rather than confront Carol, Alice discusses her complaints with Grace and swears Grace to secrecy. Equally prevalent is the temptation to complain about pastors behind their back but never confront them. At times, triangulation takes on a quasi-official form. Parishioners who meet in a private home to discuss the pastor or to complain about lay leaders are functioning with inappropriate secrecy. Church councils, vestries, sessions, or boards that hold executive sessions to discuss allegations against the pastor or parishioners in the absence of the accused parties practice damaging secrecy. Boards and committees that classify information about the state of church finances as "confidential" or suggest that meeting minutes should be available only to their members are keeping secrets. That information should be readily available to any church member.

Secrets are toxic for congregations in several ways.

1. When triangulation occurs, even the participants begin to wonder when they will become its victims. If Alice talks to Grace about Carol, Grace may wonder what Alice says about *her* to others. If parishioners, either informally or as an official body, meet in secret about a layperson, those in the meeting may worry that they might be targets of similar action if they annoy someone. That is how secrets destroy trust. When complaints are "secretly" lodged with a third party, pastors and parishioners cannot trust that they will be confronted openly and be given the opportunity to apologize for mistakes or be cleared of ill-informed accusations. Over time, this breakdown of trust will permeate the congregation. Parishioners no longer will feel comfortable talking with each other about anything but the weather.

2. When an atmosphere of secrecy shrouds boards or committees, parishioners will increasingly become reluctant to ask legitimate questions about congregational issues, lest they be labeled troublemakers. Again, trust is destroyed, and even casual conversations may become stilted.

3. Once trust is threatened, thoughtful input by parishioners is squelched. There is no arena for the exchange of ideas and options that might lead to problem resolution. Ministry is stymied because few, if any, members are willing to stick their necks out and suggest new programs or approaches.

4. Taken to its extreme, official secrecy can shield wrongdoing that needs to be exposed and corrected. The most obvious examples, which have been discussed widely elsewhere, involve clergy sexual misconduct. But other clergy and lay misbehavior may similarly be covered up by inappropriate secrecy.

Much of the time, it will be fairly easy to distinguish between legitimate confidentiality and illegitimate secrecy. But sometimes the issues are less clear. How does a healthy congregation deal with misconduct that stems from a pastor's or lay leader's painful personal problems? How can we remedy these situations without exposing the person to public humiliation? Of course, if the issue is alleged sexual or financial misconduct, immediate action must be taken to relieve the person of his or her duties temporarily until a finding of guilt or innocence is made. But other misconduct issues are more problematic.

Consider this hypothetical question posed during one workshop. One parishioner asked: "How should we handle a situation if we have a popular minister, but the deacons know he or she has a serious drinking problem?

Should the deacons take their concerns to a church council meeting? Or should they go directly to the conference minister?" In this case, the response was first to confront the pastor. If that fails to achieve a behavioral change, then go directly to the judicatory official who serves as the pastor's pastor. If that step fails, take the concerns to the appropriate judicatory disciplinary body that has the power to compel the pastor to seek help and change his or her behavior. A similar process might be undertaken with a pastor or lay leader whose emotional problems are playing out in destructive behavior within the congregation.

Determining the healthiest and most compassionate way to handle troubled clergy or laypeople is a tough call. Lay leaders understandably may want to protect the person's privacy. At the same time, if the behavior seriously threatens congregational fellowship, parishioners may need to be told by congregational leaders or denominational officials at some time what actions—such as discipline or directed counseling—have been taken to correct the problem.

In a slightly different way, parish study groups may also provide settings for inappropriate behavior. Clergy and lay leaders should be concerned when study groups seem to be verging on therapy sessions for individuals or when they become an arena for complaining about the pastor or parishioners who are not present. I heard one layperson insist that whatever is said in Bible study should remain there and not be divulged or discussed outside the group. That practice feels uncomfortable to me. No, we should not go to other parishioners and complain that Joe's theology is crazy or that Mary seems clueless when it comes to the Scriptures, basing our remarks on Joe's and Mary's participation in the Bible study. But we ought to be able to—and indeed *want* to—tell others about what we are discussing and what we are learning.

Fit congregations will encourage discussion of congregational issues and problems, will invite questions, and will widely communicate decisions. They will acknowledge problems and seek widespread participation in solving them. They will listen to thoughtful questions by parishioners and not seek to squelch "messengers" who sound alarms that something is wrong. And they will honor appropriate confidentiality but refuse to keep secrets.

Questions for Reflection

1. When problems arise in your congregation, can you talk openly about them at committee or board meetings? If so, what quality of the atmosphere in your congregation makes that possible? If not, what prevents such open discussion?

2. Has your congregation tried to repress or bury issues? What was the result?

3. Have painful problems been openly examined? What was the result?

4. When someone raises concerns in a meeting, how is the message greeted and handled? How are "messengers" who "sound alarms" treated?

5. Are you confident that your congregation can process problems and conflicts in a healthy manner? Why or why not?

6. Think about some typical congregational issues or problems. Which ones should be kept "confidential"? Which ones would be inappropriate "secrets" that ought to be discussed or communicated?

Chapter 7

BEWARE OF PLATITUDES

I'm really upset about how Gary was treated by the Christian education committee. They knocked down every idea he offered and as much as told him they could do without him.

Oh, now, we just have to move on and forget the past.

That was really a nasty exchange at the church council meeting last week. And it wasn't the first time the deacons had jumped all over the music committee.

Well, now, we just have to forgive and forget those things.

You know, we seem to keep repeating the same mistakes. We really don't listen to each other very well, and some people have really been hurt. Something is going on that needs to be put on the table and discussed.

Oh, those people just have to get over it.

Variations of the no-talk rule can even be applied after a conflict is acknowledged. Their two most frequent forms are "Just forgive and forget," and "We have to put this all behind us." Just as denial is an unhealthy way to deal with the reality of conflict, so too is the subsequent premature admonition to forgive and forget after the conflict has been acknowledged. When we insist on premature closure of a painful episode, we fail to learn the lessons that episode provided, and we may revictimize the victims.

Certainly, there does come a time when a congregation should put the conflict on the shelf. I use the term "on the shelf" because both "forgetting" and "putting it behind us" suggest that somehow what happened can and should be erased from individual and collective memories. Putting it on the shelf suggests relegating it to an appropriate spot—not out front on the desktop or bulletin board, but appropriately stored along with every other piece of the congregation's history or resources, so it will not be erased and pastors, leaders, and parishioners may in the future refer to lessons learned.

First, it may be helpful to examine what sometimes lurks behind the facile admonitions to "forgive and forget" or "put the past behind us." Chances are that few people really forgive or forget without examining the issue, although they may not openly challenge the maxim. Succumbing to the counsel of "forgive and forget" simply buries resentment and grudges a layer or two deeper. Hardly anyone forgets. Whatever it was that we were urged to forgive and forget lurks there in the midst of us, not unlike the "elephant in the living room," a staple metaphor for alcoholic family dynamics. What this means is that just about everyone knows there is this "thing," this elephant, in the middle of the room, but just about everybody pretends it is not there. Unfortunately, it takes up a lot of space and folk have to walk around it. And when new people come into the church, they may stumble over the elephant and be puzzled by its presence and the fact that no one openly acknowledges its presence.

THE NEED FOR REPENTANCE

The premature suggestion that it is time to forgive and forget ignores the need for repentance. While individuals can forgive, regardless of the behavior of the ones who harmed them, and heal personally, repentance is often a critical factor in congregational healing. As Halstead points out, forgiveness cannot be forced or demanded. Without repentance, the advice to forgive is "glib," he says, and grows out of a control-based paradigm. "Failure to accept responsibility and to confess group sin can lead to blaming the 'unforgiving' victim. . . . Trying to forgive and forget often prevents our healing enough to truly forgive and forget," he warns.[1] Too often, those who urge forgiveness and forgetting are not ready to acknowledge their roles in the conflict and hope that what they did will be forgotten without their having to make amends or offer apologies.

There are at least two problems with this approach. First, those who avoid acknowledging their roles are likely to repeat their problematic behavior in the future because they have never really faced up to and examined it. Second, as Halstead points out, the admonition simply revictimizes the victims. They were victimized first because they were wounded by unjust, perhaps even mean behavior. Now they are made to feel guilty again because they cannot just erase that wounding from their memories. Demanding forgiveness without extending repentance simply fans the frustration, hurt, and anger of those who were mistreated in the first place. Oh, the wounded may try to bury that anger and frustration for a while, but under the skin those emotions continue to rub the wound raw.

Similarly, when people prematurely advise that "we've got to put all that behind us," it may be that they have a stake in "putting it behind." Again, they may not want to own up to their own role in the conflict, or they do not want to deal with the temporary stress of thoughtfully examining what happened.

One problem with these often well-intentioned bits of advice is that they run counter to how our brains function. Psychologists tell us that we do not, indeed cannot, erase experiences or feelings from our individual or collective memories. Any doubts I might have had about the persistent presence of past experiences in my unconscious have been erased by my dreams. Over a few months, central dream characters included a woman who had cut and styled my hair when I was a teenager five decades ago and an elementary-school classmate whose name I have neither spoken nor heard for 45 years. Yet their names and faces were stored somewhere in my unconscious and surfaced in those dreams. If those innocuous folk reappear in my dreams, consider how much more unlikely it is that painful experiences and feelings will simply disappear. Instead, the harder we try to erase those experiences and feelings from our memories, the more they tend to bubble to the surface.

Here is how Halstead puts it:

> As with grief, shutting down someone's feelings of hurt in the congregation is like covering over a wound too quickly without cleansing it thoroughly. The wound does not automatically heal with time. Infection will set in and lead to problems that can spread and infect the whole congregations. If we are not open with people or groups that we feel have wronged us, or if they are not willing

to work for reconciliation when we openly share the hurt, the healing process is cut off.[2]

Halstead likens this situation to wounds that "must be cleaned, painful
though that may be, or they will heal incompletely, become infected, and
lead to more acute pain and peril later. If an emotional wound is covered
over too quickly without being cleaned out thoroughly by grief work, infec-
tion will set in and lead to bitterness, depression, physical disease, violence,
or other relational problems."[3]

Unpacking the Issues

When Douglas Walrath, a retired parish pastor, seminary professor, and
church consultant, talks about dealing with conflict, he recommends "unpacking it," a concept that makes great sense. When we unpack a box or
suitcase, we take things out, one at a time, and examine them to determine
where we want to put them. We can unpack the complex issues involved in
a conflict in much the same way, taking one piece out at a time, examining
it, and then determining where we want to store it or, perhaps, put it to
immediate use. For example, in unpacking a conflict between boards of
deacons and trustees, we may discover that the church council held executive sessions at which the deacons made allegations about trustees in the
trustees' absence. We might immediately use this discovery to develop a
policy that no board or individual be subjected to allegations in their absence. We might use this fact to state or restate that in the future we will
make sure that anyone—be it the pastor, a lay leader, or a group—is openly
confronted with any such complaints. Then we might store that item on the
shelf—perhaps in some newly written by-law or set of procedures to which
we can refer if we have any questions later.
    At the next level, we unpack just what those accusations were. Trust-
ees now have an opportunity to respond. If they did act inappropriately, they
now have a chance to apologize, be granted forgiveness, and make sure
that the inappropriate action is not repeated. If they were not guilty of the
allegations, they can be cleared. What we put on the shelf is the truth as
best we can discover it. If inaccurate gossip about this issue crops up in the
future, we can go back to the shelf and retrieve the truth to clear up the
issue. I suspect that if we follow this "unpacking procedure," by the time

we get to the bottom of the conflict bag or box, we will find it less and less stressful to deal with the individual items.

Now, to mix metaphors: When we unpack conflicts in this manner, we do not erase memories, but we do reframe them. If we have done our unpacking well, those memories may be fleshed out with more context and understanding and truth. The issue is not forgetting but deciding *what* we will remember. We can remember appropriately. If, five years in the future, we begin to encounter an issue similar to the one we unpacked, we can go to the right shelf in our stored memory and take out the lessons we learned earlier.

HOLDING THINGS MORE LIGHTLY

These platitudes are closely tied to an increasingly popular pop-psychology term—*closure*. It is frequently uttered by television news reporters interviewing crime or disaster victims. When an alleged murderer is convicted and sentenced, the victim's relatives are asked, "Does this bring closure for you?"

I began to chafe at this term when, after several months of sharing the pain of conflict in my church with friends, several began to suggest that I needed to move on and achieve closure. Each time I heard that word uttered, something in me rebelled, but I could not pinpoint that "something." They were probably right, I thought. Although my feelings about the situation and the hurt I had experienced still ran deep, maybe it was time to let go. And why did I feel this vague resentment at the suggestion that closure was now appropriate?

Shortly thereafter, following the sentencing of one of the men convicted in the 1995 bombing of the Alfred P. Murrah Federal Building in Oklahoma City, I watched as a network television reporter asked the wife of a victim if the sentencing would bring closure for her. She reacted almost angrily, saying there would never be closure for the loss of her husband. That would simply never happen. Her remarks brought me instant relief. Syndicated columnist Ellen Goodman, in a 1998 piece headlined "Hurrying Healing," voiced similar reactions. Referring specifically to the Oklahoma City bombing and generally to others who have lost loved ones, she concluded, "[W]hen the center of someone's life has been blown out like the core of a building, is it any wonder if it takes so long even to find a door to close?"[4]

Too often exhortations for closure lay guilt trips on victims. Prematurely urging closure tends to revictimize the victims of pain, whatever the source of that pain. To victims, at least, it sounds as if well-intentioned friends are saying, "Your continued pain is your fault. Just get over it." Closure, like that forgive-and-forget advice, suggests that we can simply drop the curtain on our feelings or erase them from our mind's and heart's memory. But when those feelings run deep, that is often not possible. We cannot simply expunge the feelings of grief following the death of a loved one at the end of some socially prescribed mourning period. Nor can we simply jettison feelings of betrayal and pain when we have been deeply hurt by someone or a group about whom we cared.

As Halstead points out, premature "closure" without healing through sometimes painful grief work may result in later emergence of disease (as in dis-ease)—perhaps unexplained anger, depression, illness, or addiction. I believe that process is what mental-health experts term unhealthy repression. It is likely, too, that the frustration and anger which a victim may experience by feeling forced to premature closure is added to the temporarily buried original pain. There is another reason why simplistic closure does not make a lot of sense. Again, the rudiments of psychology suggest that our personalities and identities are the sum of our cumulative life experiences and that this cumulative total includes painful as well as joyous experiences. Realistically, we can never achieve that closure which requires us to erase a painful experience from memory.

However, it is not healthy to remain in a state of perpetual wallowing and wound licking. That behavior gets us stuck in our pain. What does make more sense to me as a healthier option is an image that Sister Elizabeth Wagner suggested in another context to a class at Bangor Theological Seminary—to "hold things more lightly." Referring to Teresa of Avila's suggestions for spiritual growth, she said that one of Teresa's three principles was "perspective." Perspective, Wagner explained, really means to hold things more lightly.

I find the images of "closure" and "holding lightly" instructive. When I think of closure, I picture a closed hand, fingers curled into the palm around an object so that the object is no longer visible. I think of clutching a small, irregular stone. If it has sharp edges or an abrasive surface and anxiety causes my hand to close tightly, the act of closing becomes clenching, and the stone is likely to put painful, even cutting pressure on my palm, perhaps even producing a wound. The wound in the covered palm is invisible to others, but it continues to cause me pain.

Consider the alternative—holding the stone lightly in an open palm. Now it is visible and can be examined. It can be gently turned over and over. New glints of color and various surface textures become visible. I can caress the stone, gently feeling its various surfaces with my fingertips. At the very least, held lightly, the stone no longer cuts into my palm. While carrying it may remain a bit of a burden, it no longer is the source of unseen pain. Ultimately, I can let go of it for periods of time, perhaps placing it on a mantel or bedside table, then picking it up at times to feel its varied surfaces again until it becomes familiar, perhaps almost comfortable as a talisman of sorts.

I find great comfort in this image as I deal with painful experiences in my life. Rather than try prematurely to close such an experience in my mind and heart and press the pain inward, I can hold it more lightly, gently turn it over, and examine it more closely. As I do this, I see glints of new realities or revelations. Did a piece of this experience teach me something about myself and about how I relate to others? As I pass my spiritual thumb over it, I find some smooth spots I failed to notice before, spots where a gesture of kindness and caring became part of the total experience. Over time, I begin to let it go for a while and place it on my emotional mantel. It is still there, and at times when I am puzzled or a bit down, I can pluck it back into my mental palm to examine it again for new glints of understanding. Perhaps someday I will place it permanently on the mantel or in a jar of other stones representing other painful and joyful experiences in my life. Or perhaps I will carry it in my pocket as a talisman—to finger gently as a reminder of the healing that eventually came as I held it ever more lightly.

Questions for Reflection

1. How do you feel when someone advises you to forgive and forget something you still find quite painful?

2. When you have forgiven, what factors have made that possible?

3. Has your congregation been able to unpack problems, disagreements, or conflicts? How was that done, and how and where were the issues stored for reference? What lessons were learned that continue to serve your congregation well?

4.   Think of a past conflict in your congregation—major or minor—that was not properly examined. How might you "unpack" it and how and where would you store what you unpack?

5.   Consider some issue to which you have been advised to bring closure. How might you feel if, instead, you held it more lightly?

Chapter 8

CLEAR THE DECKS

There's a congregational meeting to vote on the new hymnal. I don't know much about it, but I do know the diaconate is supporting it. Remember when the deacons refused to invite Reverend Burke back to preach? Let's get together a lot of no votes on this hymnal thing to show them how it feels to be on the losing end.

The minister has called a meeting to reaffirm his congregational support. Those trustees are giving him a hard time, and I'm still mad at them because they refused to buy new linoleum for the kitchen. Guess I'll go and vote for the minister.

What is wrong with these scenarios? They bring old battles to new controversies. Guess what happens in these cases? Neither the old fight nor the new one gets resolved in a healthy manner. People who know little or nothing about the latent, still potent resentments are likely to be puzzled by the dynamics of the new conflict. Discussion or even arguments at meetings often make no sense to them. And individuals who are supported in the current situation by people fighting old fights are likely to misread that support.

We do not make wise decisions when we continue to act out of old resentments and old fights that are irrelevant to the issue at hand. Refighting past battles in situations totally removed from them only muddies the water because we are not able to examine the present issue clearly. Good decisions are made when we are able to isolate an issue and examine the pros and cons and in-betweens. Bad decisions result when irrelevant issues are injected into the deliberations.

Consider the implications of the first statement at the beginning of this chapter. The issue at hand is whether to purchase and use new hymnals. The deacons—and perhaps the music director, organist, and choir director—have spent weeks or even months reviewing the new hymnal, comparing it to the present one, and singing and hearing some of the newer hymns. The pastor has made a coherent theological case for the new hymnal, which the deacons and others have heard and accepted. Now it is time to explain the rationale to the entire congregation, hear the reactions and comments from other parishioners, and make a decision.

Enter Wanda Haynes, a disgruntled church member fighting an old fight. While the deacons and others have been giving thoughtful attention to the music and theology of the respective hymnals, Haynes has been rounding up friends and making her case that it is time to put those deacons in their place. She and her friends may never have examined the proposed hymnal or heard arguments supporting or opposing it. By the time the congregational meeting is held, other parishioners are likely to be so caught up in the angry emotions or confusion that they will hear little or nothing the pastor, deacons, music committee members, and music director say. The hymnal is not the issue. "Once again, those deacons are just trying to control everything," Haynes tells the assemblage. "The old hymnals are just fine." Her remarks are greeted with significant, if scattered, applause.

Newcomers are confused. They were not involved with the church when the dispute over the former pastor occurred and are unaware that Haynes and her allies have come bearing old grudges. But they can sense the tension in the room and, because they are new, they may not ask the kinds of questions that would clarify the issues and return the focus of discussion to the proposed hymnal. If it is so controversial, they reason, maybe they should vote no to keep peace. After the new-hymnal proposal is defeated, those supporting the new hymnal may conclude that they simply must do a better job of educating the congregation about its value. They will likely be frustrated when they find their efforts bearing little fruit. The bottom line is that the value of the hymnal never surfaced. It was never considered thoughtfully and honestly by most of the congregation. Those fighting the old grudges savor their victory, and others who never really understood what was going on think that they at least did their part to keep peace in the congregation.

There is a subsidiary problem with this scenario: the issue of the deacons' refusal to invite the former pastor back as a supply preacher is never resolved either. Haynes and her allies never approached the deacons directly to hear their rationale in that case. Maybe those deacons had good reasons for that previous decision and maybe they were in error. As a result, neither issue—which hymnal is best or whether Burke was treated unfairly—is ever properly addressed and resolved.

This kind of behavior—bringing old grudges to new and unrelated issues—tends to be repeated until it becomes all but impossible to sort out the grudges that are in play and the truth about any of the situations, old or new. When this behavior becomes entrenched, chances are that few, if any, issues will be considered on their merits.

MIXED MESSAGES

The other problem with fighting old fights during consideration of new and unrelated issues is that the end result may send the wrong signals to some of the "winners." Consider the second scenario cited at the chapter's beginning. Let us say that the Rev. Buster Jones has been careless in committing church money for items outside the parameters of the budget. The trustees, carrying out their responsibility, are trying to rein him in. This is not necessarily a case of clergy financial misconduct, but it needs to be addressed. Pastor Jones decides to take his case to the congregation. But Barbara Collins is still seething about the trustees' refusal to install that new kitchen linoleum. Time to teach those trustees a lesson, she reasons. So, like Haynes, she rounds up her friends—perhaps even summoning folk who seldom attend worship and have not really been active in the life of the church for several years.

When the congregation meets, the trustees try to spell out their concerns. They point out that they are charged by the congregation with financial oversight and believe that it is their responsibility to make sure spending is in line with the budget approved by the congregation. Jones counters that this is an issue of pastoral authority. The congregation hired him, and the trustees are trying to restrict him unduly. In a healthy congregation, such an exchange might spark a thoughtful discussion of pastoral and lay leader responsibilities. In a dysfunctional church family in which members come to such meetings consumed with old grudges, few people even hear what the trustees are saying. Collins and her group are poised to put down the trustees, and others are so unnerved by the tense atmosphere that they, too, hear little if any substantive discussion. Collins or one of her supporters quickly moves to back the pastor. If Collins has any significant support, again those who are unaware of the hidden agenda conclude that it is easier and safer to vote with her group. Ah—the pastor has been affirmed. Or has he?

In this case, the vote may have little or nothing to do with what the majority of the congregation thinks about the pastor, about his relationship with the trustees, or about his pastoral authority. Collins and her allies may not even like him much. The vote simply provided them with an opportunity to strike back at trustees whose previous decision Collins and her allies resent. The vote also may prove to be a hollow or, at least, misleading victory for Pastor Jones. If he understands it as support for maintaining or even increasing his power over the trustees, he may stray farther afield or simply be blindsided when he does something to offend Collins and her group. Once again, two issues remain unexamined—the balance of power and authority between the pastor and elected lay leaders, not to mention concerns about money management, and whether new linoleum should be purchased for the kitchen.

CLEAN UP YOUR CONGREGATIONAL HISTORY

Another factor that can muddy consideration of current issues is an inaccurate sense of a congregation's history. Seldom are those current issues addressed without some parishioners comparing or contrasting them to events or developments in the congregation's past. Applying incorrect understandings of the past to a present situation can lead a congregation astray.

First, it is important to recognize several forms of that history:

1. Official congregational history is often contained in commemorative booklets prepared for special events such as celebrations of a church's centennial or bicentennial. Extra copies are printed and made available to new members and clergy applying for the pastor's position. Although these histories sometimes acknowledge problems in a church's earliest years, they seldom deal forthrightly with any controversial issues within memory of present members, lest such candor upset the congregation.

2. Records of meetings of the congregation and its key boards and committees offer another historical perspective. Their accuracy and the

completeness of the information that they contain depend on who happened to be the scribe at any particular time. For example, in my own church one clerk provided lengthy, detailed accounts of congregational and church council meetings, and another recorded little more than approved motions. The former records, which include descriptions of debates or conversations preceding motions, provide church historians with some sense of context. The latter reports offer little indication of how parishioners or church council members arrived at the decisions they made. Such sketchy records can be misleading. Once again, temptation is strong to avoid recording anything in the minutes that might upset some members or seem to reflect badly on the church.

3. Often more powerful than anything written is the oral history that every congregation develops—the stories that are frequently repeated and handed on to succeeding generations. Usually, this oral history is replete with interesting and humorous anecdotes that provide entertainment at church picnics or homecoming celebrations. But often the first tellers of this history had personal agendas that colored and perhaps distorted the facts. We also have a tendency to view the past through rose-colored glasses, to recall the past only in terms of "the good old days."

A minister in his first pastorate told me about two examples of misinformation-as-history he had discovered. Parishioners talked, he said, about the glory days when the church youth group numbered 100 or more. Of course, they added, those were the days when the town's population was around 20,000, and now it is down to 8,000. My clergy friend did a little research and learned that his church's youth group had never attracted more than 25 teens. But for a time, four local churches scheduled some joint activities for youth. Together the youth from all four churches numbered 100. Then he checked census data from 1920 onward and discovered that the town had never had more than 8,600 residents.

Individuals have their own understanding of their congregation's history, and those individual understandings sometimes differ sharply. When a congregation is involved in a conflict, each side—and there may be more than two—has its own version of what happened. In one church whose dwindling membership and finances prompted parishioners to consider closing, a longtime member insisted that the downturn began when the first United Church of Christ minister was called in the late 1950s. (Founded as a Baptist church, this parish became a Congregational church in the 1920s and three decades later voted to join the newly formed UCC.) This old-timer also recalled the more recent tenure of a Baptist lay preacher as well received by the congregation. However, another longtime member recalled that the first UCC pastor was "a real ball of fire" who inspired people. She saw the Baptist lay minister's tenure as triggering the downturn.

As it turned out, a review of nearly a century's worth of Congregational and UCC yearbooks seemed to support the latter memory. According to the figures recorded in those volumes, membership began to climb soon after the first UCC minister arrived. It plummeted during the Baptist lay minister's term. If this congregation decides to revisit the issue of denominational affiliation now and takes its history into account in the deliberations, it will be important that the accepted history of this issue conform to the facts. In his book *Working the Angles: the Shape of Pastoral Integrity*, Eugene Peterson—writer, poet, and spiritual theology professor—talks about history before the Enlightenment, when it was written "with some scheme in mind." Says Peterson: "History writing ranged between the poles of propaganda and gullibility." Those writing from the propaganda pole sorted through the evidence and included only that which supported their cause. Those writing from the gullibility pole often reported simple gossip.[1] Congregations are vulnerable to the same problems. Clerks, scribes, or parish historians with personal agendas can sort through the facts and record only those that support their personal agendas. A church's oral history—those oft-repeated stories—can be riddled with gossip and run counter to documented facts, and yet be passed on to succeeding generations of parishioners.

Inaccurate church history and the fighting-old-fights behavior can create a destructive cycle that must be broken if a congregation is going to deal constructively with conflict. If pieces of a congregation's history—written or oral—are factually wrong or understood differently, they can become the foundation for fighting old fights. If issues are not examined when they arise, then misunderstandings, misinformation, or grudges become the leftover baggage that carries old fights into new and unrelated disputes. At the same time, if old disputes are never resolved, if they simply leave a destructive residue of several versions of "what happened," congregational history becomes either a piece of propaganda or a collection of gossip.

Bad history feeds fighting old fights. Fighting old fights—never addressing the present issue head-on—leads to muddled history. Fighting an earlier dispute in the midst of a new one ensures that neither is resolved. Congregations that engage in this behavior are always one or two battles behind, and the core issues of each are never addressed.

Discover Your Common Story

How can congregations break such a destructive cycle? A clergy friend put it best. After meeting with parishioners of a conflicted congregation and sensing that it lacked a coherent history, she advised the assembled parishioners that they needed "to tell a common story until everyone understands." Note that she did not say they should tell a common story until everyone agrees, but until everyone understands.

Return to that congregation whose parishioners held two conflicting views of the first UCC minister and of a subsequent Baptist lay minister. Those two longtime members will probably never agree about those two clergy. But they and the congregation can come to a common understanding. How might that common story be developed? First, regardless of how each pastor was viewed by individual parishioners, membership increased soon after the UCC pastor arrived and decreased during the Baptist lay minister's tenure. Second, each pastor had his supporters and his critics. Third, the calling of a UCC pastor did not trigger the church's decline. And finally, some parishioners are not comfortable with the UCC. The commonly understood story might be something like this:

> Some of us really liked our first UCC minister, and some of us did not. There was a similar difference of opinion about the later Baptist pastor. The church grew under the UCC minister and declined under the Baptist pastor. But among parishioners some disagreement remains as to whether we should remain a UCC congregation or revert to our Baptist roots.

Perhaps the issue this congregation needs to examine, then, is its denominational affiliation. Speakers might provide some education about United Church of Christ and Baptist polity, how each denomination relates to local congregations—and then a congregational forum could be held where parishioners can voice their views. They may conclude that another denomination would better fit their collective theology and identity. Or the majority of members may decide that they want to continue the UCC affiliation, and those who remain dissatisfied may want to seek a faith community more in line with their own theology. Arriving at a commonly understood story can clarify issues and lead to productive discussions and, ultimately, to sound decisions.

If there is leftover baggage from old fights, it should be acknowledged and clarified. Often people with historic axes to grind lack enough accurate information about the old fight to develop an informed opinion. I have heard grumbling about some of those old fights in my own congregation from people who were not involved in those discussions, knew little to nothing about their content, and reacted only to the results. Not every ancient battle can or should be disinterred. Some may be so old that no one remains in the congregation with any firsthand observations. However, it may be prudent to examine more recent ones that seem to have spawned continuing grudges—perhaps by assembling those who were involved or who observed the old battle firsthand to develop a commonly understood story.

KEEP FOCUSED

The most important action that a fit congregation can take is to insist that current discussions remain focused on the issues at hand and that the substance of the debate be accurately recorded. What are some healthy habits laypeople can develop to accomplish this?

1. When a dispute or difficult discussion arises, the chair, moderator, or whoever presides can be firm about setting aside issues that have little or nothing to do with the one at hand. Individual participants in the discussion or responsible bystanders similarly can be attentive to this process. If they think the conversation is drifting to an unrelated subject, they can point that out and direct attention back to the current issue. If the dispute is particularly contentious or emotionally charged, the person presiding might even appoint someone to monitor the discussion for relevance. It is not always obvious that unrelated issues or old grudges are at play in a discussion. However, trained listeners may pick up some signals:

a. *Non sequiturs.* If one speaker is addressing the current issue and the next speaker begins to talk about a totally different subject, focus is lost.

b. *Sweeping generalizations.* If the issue is a proposed new hymnal and someone interjects, "The deacons never listen to us," the focus has changed from specific discussion of the hymnal to more generalized remarks about the deacons' accountability to the congregation.

c. *Premature calls for a vote.* If someone calls the question—for a vote—before a matter has been thoroughly discussed or examined, before everyone has had at least one opportunity to speak, chances are that some folk came with an unrelated agenda that they hope to carry out via the vote.

d. *The obvious.* Wanda Haynes interjects, "Why should we listen to the deacons when they wouldn't invite Reverend Burke to fill the pulpit?" The hymnal issue has been shoved aside.

2. If serious unrelated side-disputes surface, do not simply ignore them. To do so will frustrate and probably anger those who brought them up. Instead, the chair or an appointed monitor can schedule a separate opportunity to deal with the side issue. If the comments by Haynes and her friends indicate some serious disagreement with the deacons, firmly propose that they attend the next deacons' meeting to discuss how supply pastors are chosen. Now both issues will get a fair hearing—the proposed hymnal at the congregational meeting and the decision about Smith at the deacons' meeting.

3. Restate the essence of what a previous speaker has said to that speaker's satisfaction. Doing so may be prudent in any case because in congregational meetings, some parishioners may either not hear everything another says or may filter what was heard through their own agendas and conclude something quite different from what was said.

4. Provide each parishioner attending the meeting with an agenda and printed material relating to the issue to be considered. For a meeting about proposed new hymnals, someone might develop a written list of the merits and shortcomings of that hymnal, or the pros and cons of both old and new hymnals. For a meeting about reining in the pastor's spending, parishioners might be provided with a copy of the by-laws and descriptions of the pastor's and trustees' responsibilities.

STICK TO THE FACTS

Similarly, laypeople can take some critical steps to improve the accuracy of their congregation's written and oral history.

1. Board and committee scribes and secretaries can be instructed to provide a summary of the discussion that precedes significant motions. That summary should include both supporting and opposing views. Such summaries provide the important context that will help subsequent generations understand the real reasons for an action.

2. Each board or committee can be scrupulous about reading and correcting meeting minutes before approving them for the official record.

3. In parking-lot or telephone conversations about alleged actions by the pastor or boards and committees, parishioners can urge each other to go to the best source for accurate information.

4. Parishioners who have unwittingly conveyed erroneous information can correct it. A simple telephone call to say, "Hey, I got that wrong—I've read the minutes [talked to the chair] and discovered this is what really happened," will gain that parishioner more respect than sticking with the wrong account.

5. Schedule a potluck supper to develop a congregational historical time line. This exercise is often employed by professional conflict managers, but parishioners can carry it out as well. This exercise can be particularly useful if the official written history or deeply embedded oral history of a congregation departs significantly from actual experience. The leader simply stretches a long strip of butcher paper across the front of the room and marks off years or decades. In all but the largest congregations, parishioners might first be asked to come forward and write their names under the year they first began attending the church. This action provides them with a sense of ownership of the process and the result. Then parishioners are asked to name high and low points in the church's life—when a particularly gifted pastor served the church, when a building addition was completed, when there was an especially hurtful dispute, when a poorly prepared or emotionally impaired minister served, when the Sunday school attendance was highest, when a pledge or other financial campaign was particularly successful or unsuccessful.

The leader might provide a head start by reviewing records and noting the church membership numbers at various times over the previous 50 years.[2] I did a mini-version of this exercise with one congregation, assembling annual membership and financial contribution figures over a half-century and then sitting down with two longtime parishioners to seek explanations for significant increases and decreases. Each offered some information that was news to the other, even though both had been involved with the church at the same junctures in question. Similarly, parishioners participating in this exercise on a congregation-wide basis may learn new things about their church's history. The exercise may also dispel some of that erroneous oral history. For example, a particular membership decline may have had little or nothing to do with the pastor then serving. Instead, someone may point out, the year membership took a precipitous dip may have been the same year a local textile plant closed and many parishioners moved away to find jobs.

6. Finally, perhaps after such a time line is developed (and kept on file for future reference), parishioners may discover a need to develop one or more of those common stories about particularly contentious items. Perhaps a pastor who served 20 years ago is viewed in controversial and contradictory ways by parishioners. Some saw him as caring and challenging; others felt ignored by him and thought his sermons were too radical. As a result, some parishioners left the church, and others retained residual anger or emotional pain. The common story might be just that—that this pastor was well-liked by some and heartily disliked by others, and the resulting disagreements caused some to leave and others to experience long-term pain. Period. That describes the situation without blaming anyone and, just maybe, brings some closure.

As I suggested earlier, you can expect to experience differences of opinion, disputes, and even contentious conflicts in your congregation if it is alive and open to the Holy Spirit. Fit congregations will discover that these encounters can be healthy challenges to follow Christ—to be more caring of each other, to reach out to others, to stretch themselves spiritually—if their focus is clear and uncluttered by old fights and if their history is a story that everyone understands.

Questions for Reflection

1. What unresolved disputes in your congregation might foster leftover grudges?

2. What does your written history (booklets, pamphlets) say about the life of this congregation? Does it accurately reflect your understanding? Were painful developments omitted?

3. Think of a meeting whose stated purpose got lost in emotional dialogue or subject shifting. How might thoughtful parishioners have directed the conversation back on track?

4. Are there often-repeated but conflicting oral stories about your congregation's past? How might you rewrite that oral history to reflect a common understanding of what happened?

5. Examine minutes of the last two or three congregational meetings. If you were a pastor or parishioner in the year 2030, would you have an accurate reflection of what happened from those minutes? If not, how might these records be improved?

Chapter 9

EXORCISE THE GHOSTS

I'm fairly new here, but I get the feeling that people walk on eggshells in this church.

I joined this church after attending several congregational meetings. They were so refreshing. Lots of people participated in the discussion, and some real tough questions were asked, but nobody got mad. This feels like a real safe place to be myself.

Soon after the interim pastor arrived at my church, he asked the ushers to stop dimming the chandelier lights in the sanctuary just before his sermon. I suppose he reasoned that dimming the lights might lull some folk to sleep. Why had we dimmed the lights in the first place? I thought that perhaps this practice directed parishioners' attention to the pulpit. Others thought it might have been instituted during the energy crisis. All that fellow parishioners could say now was "We've always done it that way." No, one longtime usher said, years ago a parishioner complained that the bright light bothered his eyes, so when full chandelier light was not needed, it was dimmed. The man who made that request had not worshiped in my church for six or seven years, but the light dimming continued, and except for that usher no one could recall why it was done. That is an innocuous example of the ghosts that can live on in a congregation long after the original reason for their existence has been forgotten.

Although grudges remaining from old battles may be articulated and obvious to longtime members, that is often not the case with these congregational ghosts. And the ghosts are not always as benign as that light-dimming routine. Congregations that have observed the no-talk rule are likely to find more harmful ghosts lurking in sanctuary and parish-house corners. Congregational attitudes, outlooks, and behaviors get passed on from one era to the next. The players may change, but the behaviors and attitudes often remain. It is not that some protocol is handed out to new members in written material or stated in informal conversation. Instead, the ghosts are part of the pervasive atmosphere that almost every newcomer eventually senses and then unconsciously joins.

INHERITED BEHAVIORS

Congregations with healthy inherited behavior patterns generally thrive. Their parishioners feel both cherished and challenged. Newcomers quickly sense that openness, honesty, and mutual respect are honored. They hear spirited conversations at board and committee meetings where issues of substance are tackled. They hear parishioners agreeably disagree on occasion and find ways either to compromise or to live with differences. Congregations with unhealthy behavior patterns often experience repeated cycles of disruptive and even destructive conflict, which emit an aura or undercurrent of unease—what I call "ghosts." Often, the problem for these churches is difficulty in acknowledging these ghostly inheritances; however, they must be acknowledged before they can be exorcised. It is difficult to accept that changing the players does not necessarily change the behavior, especially when no one consciously recognizes, much less talks about, the dysfunctional "rules."

When first confronted with this reality, many parishioners will vehemently deny it. "Hey, we've got 200 members, and only three or four were even here when we had all that trouble back 40 years ago," Many are likely to insist, "Most folks here now don't even know anything about it." The funny thing is, they are right, in a way. In fact, absolutely nobody may be left from the days when "that trouble" happened. But how was "that trouble" handled? "Oh, well, we just didn't talk about it," parishioners will respond. "After all, we needed to put it behind us and move on."

Here is what is important. That 40-year-old "trouble" is not the issue. Not talking about it and failing to clear the decks at the time may very well be the issue, the ghostly inheritance. Members then got the message that talking openly about difficult situations was discouraged. They did not have to deliberately pass on that message to members who joined in subsequent decades. The new members simply sensed it, perhaps subconsciously, so that when the next "trouble" occurred, they knew they were expected to keep their mouths shut and paper it over. Avoidance became ingrained in that congregational culture. No one has to tell you that walking nude down Main Street is a no-no (streaking excepted). You just know that it is a taboo because good people, acceptable people, nice people do not walk nude down Main Street. That is part of our culture.

SOME GHOSTLY AURAS

Consider these congregational ghosts:

• Parishioners at Maple Street Church obsess about money. They have a hefty endowment, and they do not begin to spend the interest. Instead, the endowment just grows year after year. Nevertheless, lay leaders periodically warn the pastor that they may not be able to keep him on a full-time basis because the local shoe plant closed and pledges are down. More laity time is spent on watchdogging endowment investments than on any other aspect of church life, including worship, Sunday school, and mission projects.

This situation makes no sense to newcomers, but any questions they ask about the practice of growing the endowment at the expense of ministry are greeted with chilly stares. If someone—a new pastor or curious layperson—has the courage to ask some questions, he or she may learn that 40 years ago, the church treasurer walked off with $50,000 of the church's money. For a while, it looked as though the church might have to close. Then Dowager Dora died and left the church a big chunk of change. While the immediate financial crunch was erased, the fears of impending financial doom remained. Those feelings became part of the congregational culture. The resultant underlying unease was passed on. Hardly anybody ever talks about that scoundrel treasurer anymore and, if you mention her, members say, "Oh, that was a long time ago." But the congregational distrust spawned by her theft lives on.

• The session (governing board) at Mercy Presbyterian Church keeps its minister on a tight rein. Session members insist on knowing where she is on her days off. They are reluctant to provide continuing-education time, and they want her day-to-day vacation itinerary with phone numbers where she can be reached. "Gee," a new member puzzles, "don't you trust her?"

"Of course we trust her," session members insist. In fact, parishioners really like this minister. She has been good about making pastoral calls, especially when parishioners are ill, in the hospital, or just down in the dumps.

If someone probes this issue, they may learn from a longtime member that 30 years ago the church had a minister who was hardly ever available. It was a tough time, too. Mary's husband died, and the minister had gone on a long-weekend fishing trip without notifying anyone. Jim's parents were in a horrible accident, and Sarah had a heart attack, and the minister was off somewhere and failed to leave word with anyone about how he could be reached. He was seldom in the office, and he made few calls. In fact, he seemed to think that all he had to do was show up on Sunday. Of course, since that minister left, the church had been blessed by very conscientious pastors, and there really have been no problems of that sort in the intervening years. So what is going on? A ghost is lurking in the shadows—the ghost of separation anxiety. Mary may be in a nursing home now, Jim has moved out of state, and Sarah passed on ages ago. But Mary's daughter still lives in town, as does Jim's sister, and a number of others who, at least subconsciously, remember that disturbing sense of facing emotional trauma without pastoral support. No one at Mercy Church actually says, "We learned a lesson. We've got to make sure we know where the minister is at all times." Instead, the undercurrent of anxiety just gets passed on, absorbed by new members as they fit into the congregational culture. They just come to accept that in this church, laypeople keep a sharp eye on the minister. If you asked session members why they are so concerned about the pastor's whereabouts, chances are they would not or could not peg their unreasoned concern to the minister who served 30 years ago. They just know that they feel uneasy when the minister isn't reachable.

These are the ghosts—avoidance, mistrust, separation anxiety—that must be exorcised if these congregations are to exchange unhealthy habits for healthy behavior. We layfolk resist acknowledging such ghosts, because admitting that we, even unintentionally, still practice these bad habits makes us feel guilty. After all, we did nothing wrong. We were not even here when these bad things—the "trouble," the theft, or the pastor's frequent absences—happened. And nobody has talked about those situations for years. Give us a break!

Probing Our Collective Subconscious

We need help—the kind of help that mental-health therapists provide when they nudge troubled individuals to recall childhood experiences, long buried in the unconscious, that trigger anxiety or acting out decades later. We need someone—the pastor, a skilled lay leader or an outside consultant—to keep asking us, lovingly but firmly, the questions whose answers will help us understand why we behave in certain ways. Thoughtful laypeople can begin this process. Actually, it is just a matter of applying common sense. When something seems to make no sense—concern that the church can no longer afford a full-time pastor when annual endowment interest alone would more than cover the salary and benefits—it is time to ask, "What is going on here?" When lay leaders seem to be micromanaging a gifted, responsible, and responsive pastor, it is time to ask, "What is that all about?" When the untuneable old piano takes up sanctuary space needed for the bell choir, it is time to ask, "Why?" (Chances are that the piano was donated by a powerful church member 60 years ago and took on the aura of an untouchable icon.)

With skillful leadership and God's grace, we may begin to unravel the conundrums. "I did get the feeling that I had to tread very carefully here and not ask a lot of questions," one newer member may offer. "Yeah," another contributes. "I've been in this church for 15 years and, come to think of it, it's always been that way." And just maybe a longtime member may be jolted to say, "Well, I wasn't here at the time, but my neighbor left the church in 1950 when that trouble happened. She doesn't say much about it, and when I asked Bruce and Kerry about it, they said, 'Just leave well enough alone.'" Finally, a brave soul might interject, "Gee, isn't it time we begin talking things out? It might really clear the air. It seems we've just gotten in the habit of covering things up, and that makes everybody tentative and a little bit uneasy." Presto—the exorcism has begun.

If these ghostly legacies seem excessively negative, consider the second comment at the beginning of this chapter. In that congregation, where discussion flows easily and respectfully, even about difficult issues, no avoidance ghost was allowed to take up residence, or that ghost was exorcised long ago. No one has to tell newcomers that this is an open, comfortable congregation, although longtime parishioners may share that message. The important thing is that the openness and comfort are obvious in just about everything this congregation undertakes—from planning the Christmas pageant to handling a budget crisis or even coping with a troubled pastor. You can sense that this congregation practices what it preaches. No, it is not perfect, but it takes its problems in stride. This is a fit congregation.

Flabby congregations can move to fitness when they acknowledge and expose those ghosts, when they bring to the surface of collective consciousness the long-ago reasons that bad habits became entrenched, and then replace them with good habits.

Questions for Reflection

1. How did you learn what behavior is expected of parishioners in your congregation? Did someone tell you, or did you just sense it? What are some of those behaviors?

2. Are there behaviors in your congregational culture that puzzle you? How were they inherited? How might you initiate some dialogue to examine the origins of those behaviors and to discuss whether continuing them makes sense?

3. What are some healthy behaviors your congregation practices? How did they evolve? How are they reinforced?

Chapter 10

WHAT ABOUT THE PASTOR?

This minister has to go. We hear enough about homosexuality and abusive husbands and supposed hate crimes during the week. We don't need to listen to sermons about those awful subjects on Sunday morning. We'll never get new members if people think that we deal with these weird things.

The minister told us she won't visit Joe and Mary and Herbert and Charlene and a dozen others, and that's it. No explanation.

Reverend Morris, we deacons need to know whom you visited this past month and what you talked about.

The minister is gone again. He said he was taking continuing education time, but he refused to say what he'll be doing. Well, I guess he's the boss.

One of the thorniest challenges congregations face is developing, maintaining, and implementing clear, fair ways to hold ministers appropriately accountable while properly respecting their rightful pastoral authority. When congregations do neither, both pastors and parishioners are hurt. In fact, a significant portion of congregational conflict focuses on some variation of authority and accountability issues.

Make no mistake about it. This area of congregational life is a virtual minefield. How does a congregation properly respect the minister's legitimate pastoral authority and, at the same time, legitimately hold the minister accountable for meeting the congregation's reasonable expectations and needs? Developing and maintaining that delicate balance between authority and accountability requires wisdom, courage, and an unflinching commitment to fairness—qualities that can too easily become lost in the midst of conflict.

First, it is important to understand the two concepts.

AUTHORITY

Authentic pastoral authority ultimately derives from credibility and trustworthiness. Clergy coming to congregations are welcomed with an initial assumption of credibility. Many have completed a fairly rigorous seminary program. They are expected to be biblically literate and to be able to reflect theologically on the intersection of Scripture and prayer with their parishioners' life situations and experiences. Moreover, clergy are assumed to have a sense of calling and to engage in sufficient spiritual discipline to be thoughtful, responsible preachers and teachers. However, authentic pastoral authority ultimately develops as parishioners come to trust clergy through experience with them. Over time, parishioners will trust their pastoral leadership if their ministers provide thoughtful preaching, wise guidance to committees, compassionate care to those seeking a pastoral presence in times of crisis, and if they maintain sound relationships with parishioners and generally make good decisions. Authentic pastoral authority is not synonymous with control. Clergy who mistake the latter for the former are asking for trouble. In addition, they are failing to carry out a key clergy task—that of empowering laity to greater ministry. A helpful resource for understanding this concept is *Growing in Authority—Relinquishing Control: A New Approach to Faithful Leadership*, by Celia Allison Hahn.[1]

ACCOUNTABILITY

Although congregations employ clergy, the pastor or rabbi in a healthy congregation is not treated like just any other employee. It makes no sense and is, in fact, demeaning, to expect a pastor to punch a time clock. Most clergy devote more than 40 hours a week to their jobs, including hours outside the nine-to-five weekday schedule. Because clergy must also respect the confidences that parishioners and others share with them, they cannot be expected to document and discuss with congregational boards or committees the content of every pastoral visit or office encounter. At the same time, clergy must be accountable for their performance in some manner. If they are not, there are two dangers: either they may function as loose cannons, doing considerable harm and straying far afield from the reasonable theological expectations of their congregation; or they may take undue advantage of a congregation by devoting very little time to the work of the church. I know of one church whose former pastor, newly ordained, insisted on a quasi-Pentecostal worship style and theology that was totally alien to that congregation's Methodist tradition and experience. At the same time, I am aware of other churches whose pastors declined to visit parishioners, even when pastoral visits were requested, or spent most afternoons on the golf course or writing books. In none of these cases were the pastors properly accountable to their congregations.

Fit congregations have processes in place to make clear which committee or board is responsible for day-to-day pastoral accountability—deacons, vestry, session, or church council. This does not mean that lay groups should micromanage ministers, since effective clergy require a good bit of latitude. But ministers will benefit if they know to whom they must answer. Further, damaging conflict often can be avoided if parishioners know to whom they should voice concerns.

The bottom line is that parish clergy are neither typical "employees" nor corporate CEOs. That is what makes congregational oversight so difficult, because too often parishioners have nothing to guide their oversight except these secular models. There is an obvious reason why we layfolk lack more appropriate models for clergy accountability. While clergy have many resources—seminary classes, books, and workshops—for exploring the accountability issue, laypeople have few. It may be helpful to examine some of the most common issues that arise around clergy performance.

POTENTIAL PROBLEM AREAS

Preaching

Some "calls" or contracts between congregations and clergy guarantee pastors freedom of the pulpit. Think of that concept as a theological first amendment. That is, if ministers are to perform an authentic prophetic role, they must be free to challenge their congregations in ways that sometimes make parishioners uncomfortable, uneasy, and occasionally angry. That certainly was the case in the 1960s when some clergy called their congregations to account on issues of racial justice—because God calls us to seek justice. There have been other hot-button issues. Some years ago one congregation voted to fire a pastor immediately, after he preached a "peace" sermon on the Sunday of Memorial Day weekend. Clergy who raise issues of peace in communities that are home to major defense contractors face anger from parishioners, as do those who preach about environmental ethics in communities where pollution-producing factories employ many residents. Even a standard stewardship sermon can draw ire. Today, perhaps the touchiest sermons may deal with issues related to homosexuality.

If we expect our clergy to live out their call, preaching and teaching the Gospel, we cannot expect an unending series of feel-good sermons. Jesus' parables and encounters invariably challenged listeners and observers to rethink what was then conventional wisdom. Jesus spoke directly to women on numerous occasions, a behavioral taboo in his time. He even overturned the moneychangers' tables in the temple. He challenged his disciples as well as the Pharisees. It follows that a fit congregation will understand and respect the minister's call to preach sermons that challenge our conventional thinking—especially when our thinking is at odds with the Gospel.

At the same time, preaching can be abusive. A minister who uses the pulpit to work out his or her own problems is abusing the congregation. Ministers understandably often use examples from their own experiences to illustrate sermon points. Some of the most effective sermons I have heard included references to the preacher's own foibles, often with a healthy dose of humor. But clergy who devote an inordinate amount of sermon time to their own physical and emotional problems or those of their families abuse their congregations.

Similarly, clergy who regularly use the pulpit to promote a secular political or economic position are out of line. This is a difficult area. What may sound like a "political" issue to some is an appropriately theological one for others. Some might find any preaching on justice issues purely "political," whereas others will argue that God's repeated scriptural calls for justice compel faithful clergy to address justice issues in our time. However, pastoral exhortations to vote for specific parties or candidates should sound clear warning signals.

Use of Time

We have all heard the old saw that ministers' lives are easy. After all, they work only on Sundays—and only Sunday mornings, at that. This is another tough area. Few if any other *employed* people work in situations comparable to those of clergy. Unlike many doctors, lawyers, consultants, and self-employed carpenters or plumbers, clergy are hired and paid by congregations. But unlike educators, business executives, cashiers, or just about any other employees, ministers set their own working schedules. How can lay leaders allow clergy appropriate latitude to carry out their responsibilities while providing the legitimate oversight that parishioners—who pay clergy salaries—have a right to expect?

First, congregations should understand that parish ministry is not a nine-to-five occupation. Among the tasks a parish pastor performs in any given week are sermon preparation, study, worship service planning (selection of hymns, liturgies, responsive readings, children's stories, prayers), home or hospital visiting, counseling sessions, newsletter preparation, staff supervision, attendance at committee and board meetings, leadership of Bible or other study groups, perhaps presence at an ecumenical meeting with other local clergy, or a regional denominational meeting. Moreover, the pastor may conduct a funeral or wedding or premarital counseling, take a turn leading worship at a local nursing home, or go to the hospital on an emergency call. Finally, there are the dozens of minor but time-consuming administrative chores—responding to phone calls, making sure the church is open for a concert or community meeting, touching base with various lay leaders. Congregations should also understand that clergy should not be expected to be on call 24 hours a day, seven days a week, 52 weeks a year.

One helpful way to look at the pastor's use of working time is in terms of units. A *unit* is any part of a morning, afternoon, or evening. For example, if a pastor spent a morning in her office answering mail and phone calls and planning worship, an afternoon visiting three parishioners, and even an hour at any evening board meeting, she would have worked three units that day. A fair workweek for a full-time pastor is ten to 14 units, depending on the season and situation. Some weeks—during Advent or Lent or when a number of parishioners are facing crises—might require 16 or more units. But the pastor should then be able to work shorter hours the following week—perhaps only six to eight units. Many employees, after all, are given compensatory time if they are not paid overtime rates for extra hours. The unit scenario may help parishioners understand why they see their pastor pulling weeds in the garden or teeing up at the golf course on a Wednesday afternoon or occasionally taking an extra day off. It is a good bet that the pastor's schedule that week included two or three night meetings and a Saturday wedding.

Conflicts over clergy use of time often focus on two issues—office presence and visitation. Pastors and their congregations sometimes disagree on the value of the pastor's spending significant time in the church office, for example. Parishioners expecting to find the pastor in the church office each weekday or at least each weekday morning may feel cheated when the pastor fails to keep that kind of schedule. At the same time, some pastors think their time is better spent working in the office only when necessary, and otherwise making hospital calls and home visits. This is especially true in parishes with a significant number of elderly or homebound members.

To avoid conflicts over the office-hours issue, this subject should be discussed when clergy candidates appear before search committees. The resolution may depend, in part, on congregational habits. In one parish, parishioners may be accustomed to the pastor's presence in the office. They know they can drop in and, if the pastor is not otherwise occupied, have a chat. This may be especially useful if parishioners are not very assertive. They may not intentionally seek counseling, but may rely on the minister to sense when they drop in that they have something they need to talk about. Some pastors, as well, find this kind of casual, open-door ministry comfortable and effective. On the other hand, pastors who feel strongly about using their time to respond to out-of-office needs may help educate their congregations on the wisdom of making advance appointments. The point here is to talk about this issue and negotiate a comfortable policy that is then communicated to the congregation.

Issues related to visiting and counseling can also be dicey. The very nature of pastor-parishioner contacts and conversations often implies an intimate sharing of feelings and concerns that parishioners wish to keep confidential. Thus, it is unreasonable and inappropriate to insist that pastors report to any lay group the names of everyone they visit or counsel and the nature of those conversations. It is not unreasonable to ask pastors to report, over the course of a month, how many pastoral visits or counseling contacts they have had. Generally, lay leaders will sense when pastors are responsibly handling visitation and counseling. They will hear positive comments about clergy visits and even some general praise for the pastor's wise counsel and good listening skills. They will also sense when something is wrong. If they hear that the pastor consistently fails to respond to requests for visits or appointments, there is a legitimate problem.

Sometimes, in the midst of congregational conflicts that focus on clergy, ministers may begin avoiding contact with those whom they believe to be their critics. In *The Pastor's Survival Manual*, Kenneth Alan Moe talks about the pastor's role in "conflict avoidance." Clergy, Moe says, "may intentionally withdraw from parishioners for brief periods of time to avoid creating or exacerbating conflict, but tact must be exercised and the interval must be short. Over extended periods, however, pastors must re-engage with their congregations, regardless of how painful, embarrassing, or unpleasant that may be."[2] There may also be isolated cases in which a pastor honestly thinks he or she cannot provide healthy, faithful counsel to a parishioner, perhaps because of an inherent personality clash. In such a case, the pastor should volunteer to secure alternate pastoral care.

Rest and Relaxation

Precisely because clergy are called to work irregular and often long hours, they need reasonable time away from the job for physical and spiritual regeneration. Some parishioners, though, balk at the four weeks of clergy vacation that have become standard for many churches. Perhaps, in their own employment, they cannot earn that much vacation until they have been on the job for ten years or more, and so they begrudge granting the pastor generous vacation time. However, few laypeople—with the possible exception of physicians—are required to work the long and irregular hours that we expect of ministers. Moreover, few ministers have the luxury of regularly having two days off in a row. Many, in fact, put in several Saturday hours polishing sermons, work most of Sunday, and then take Monday off. Clergy also need their own sources of spiritual nourishment. We layfolk are nourished each Sunday during worship. But the pastor, who leads worship, does not derive the same benefit from those services. Fit congregations will encourage their pastors to seek their own spiritual refreshment.

Pastors and their congregations benefit from clergy continuing-education programs—workshops, seminars, or retreats that help ministers grow professionally and allow them to exchange war stories with colleagues.

Again, some congregations balk at providing additional time away for pastoral continuing education, somehow feeling that it is just more vacation. However, when we laypeople are dispatched to professional conferences, we are usually paid our salaries, and our conference and travel expenses are covered by our employers. Congregations can avoid unnecessary conflict around these issues by negotiating vacation, continuing-education, and sabbatical time at the beginning of a pastor's term and putting it in writing for all parishioners to see and approve.

Decision Making

The degree to which the pastor and the congregation, as a whole or through elected lay leaders, share in making decisions about the church's administration and ministry depends on specific denominational polity. For example, in the Presbyterian tradition, the pastor chairs committees, while in the United Church of Christ and Methodist traditions, most boards and committees are chaired by laypeople. The decision-making balance between pastor and lay leaders also depends on the by-laws, traditions, and expectations of individual congregations. Some congregations may prefer to leave many decisions to the pastor, while others, with a long history of strong lay leadership, may view the pastor mostly in an ex officio role when it comes to conducting congregational business.

Unless those expectations are clearly spelled out, preferably in the congregation's by-laws and call to the pastor, unnecessary or even hurtful conflict may result. If decision making is handled solely by the pastor or solely by laity, conflict is likely to result. If lay leaders make most of the decisions, barely consulting the minister, the pastor may rightfully feel that his or her pastoral authority is not duly respected. On the other hand, if the pastor makes most of the key decisions without consulting lay leaders, parishioners may feel that their gifts and needs are being ignored.

Each congregation must come to its own terms around this issue. However, the model most frequently cited as healthy is a shared ministry that recognizes and celebrates everyone's gifts. In fact, a number of authorities predict that the future health of congregations will depend significantly on an empowered laity. Clergy who have completed rigorous seminary training bring to their position biblical literacy, theological perspectives, worship leadership skills, and sometimes administrative skills. Laypeople bring their own gifts—an understanding of and appreciation for the congregation, its diverse interests and outlooks and needs, and their own rich life experiences. Although the specific pastor-congregation power balance depends on denominational polity and individual church tradition, extremes in either direction provide potential for damaging conflict.

Congregations that effectively eliminate clergy from meaningful participation in decision-making are likely to experience a series of short-term pastorates. Ministers are not likely to remain in positions in which their gifts cannot be effectively employed and respected. Conversely, congregations whose pastors regularly shut out lay leaders from authentic participation in decision-making are likely to feel uneasy and frustrated. More important, they are vulnerable to clergy abuse. Again, conflict is this area can be minimized by clear, written policies.

Finances

Veteran clergy and divinity school professors frequently warn seminarians to stay away from the money. They advise prospective clergy to decline any process in which they have general access to church funds. Often, churches do provide clergy with limited discretionary funds that can be used for short-term confidential assistance to needy parishioners or others in the community, but it is prudent for clergy to maintain a healthy distance from general operating funds and endowments.

Less clear is the role clergy should play in general oversight of congregational financial health. While some suggest that clergy leave the entire issue to elected lay leaders or church employees such as the office manager or financial secretary, others maintain that clergy should be able to read complex financial reports and, along with trustees or other designated lay committees, oversee the financial side of church life. Clergy, these authorities argue, should be aware of potential shortfalls and of diminished contributions.

Fit congregations will have solid lay involvement in and oversight of financial affairs. While pastors will feel called to preach occasionally about the qualities of faithful stewardship, they should not be held responsible for their congregations' financial health. One almost sure-fire way to guarantee nasty and stressful conflicts is to hire pastors with either explicit or implicit expectations that they will "earn" their salaries by bringing in new members and encouraging more generous pledges. Clergy are called to preach and teach, to nurture parishioners' relationships with God. It is the congregation's responsibility to provide the financial support. I am aware of several instances in which pastors were called with such money-raising expectations. When significant additional revenues failed to materialize, these ministers were blamed.

A related issue is whether the pastor should know who contributes how much to the church. Most of my lay acquaintances respond with a clear no. Two issues are involved here. First, some financially struggling parishioners will feel embarrassed if the pastor knows that they are not tithing or otherwise giving a significant amount to the church. Others of more comfortable means who give accordingly do not want attention called to their exemplary stewardship. And some people of means would be embarrassed if the pastor knew how little they give.

Some people suggest that clergy should know what parishioners give because that giving is an indicator of spiritual well-being. A change in a member's giving, they reason, might be the signal that an issue needs to be addressed. But others fear that the pastor might respond more quickly and compassionately to the needs and opinions of the most generous givers. Clergy, as well, may want to avoid even the suspicion that their response to parishioners is based on such knowledge and, for that reason, they may prefer not to know how much each parishioner or parish family pledges.

However, lay leaders should keep ministers generally informed of their congregation's financial situation. When funds are tight, pastors may have good suggestions for cost-cutting moves. If contributions take a significant dip, that may signal other problems—some underlying congregational unrest—requiring the pastor's attention. The important point to remember, though, is that providing the necessary financial support for congregations is essentially the responsibility of the laity.

PEDESTAL PERILS

Striking a sound balance between authority and accountability when it comes to clergy requires maintaining a healthy perspective about the importance of the minister. An interim pastor of my church once said that problems arise when congregations become overfocused on the pastor. If things are going well, a congregation can become too dependent on the minister.

If things go awry, the minister is the easiest person to blame. Either way, the problem is overfocus. Avoiding that trap is not easy. After all, during each worship service, most if not all parishioners' eyes are focused on the pastor in the pulpit for an hour or more. The pastor will be present at more meetings than any one layperson. And the pastor gets paid. The laity are volunteers.

Perhaps the best way to avoid overfocusing on the pastor is to toss out the pedestal—that place atop which we layfolk are tempted to place a new minister or a long-term one who has served us well. Consider some liabilities of the pedestal.

- Clergy who are placed on pedestals by their congregations may be viewed as almost superhuman icons. People on pedestals are seldom allowed any perceptible flaws. As a result, occupants of pedestals are granted little slack for personal problems, for days when their stamina ebbs, for times when they are a bit down and cannot summon the emotional energy to be wholly positive, cheerful, and attentive to the needs of others without distractions.

- Clergy who occupy pedestals are asking for trouble. Those who bask in the unqualified affirmation and adoration encouraged by such a position seldom acknowledge or realize that they are begging for a fall. Living up to pedestal expectations can place enormously unhealthy stress on pastors. Repressed emotions, doubts, and mistakes are a prescription for all manner of physical ills and, ultimately, depression, burnout, or some other disabling emotional condition.

- A minister's fall from a pedestal can trigger significant spiritual pain for parishioners. A pastor viewed as an icon too often becomes identified with God in the minds and hearts of some parishioners, rather than as a fallible instrument of God's grace. When the pastor slips, parishioners who equate the pastor with God may begin to doubt God.

- The pedestal is a dangerous place, too, because it precludes mutual care. Certainly pastors are employed by congregations to provide pastoral care to parishioners. But it is hard to reach a member's hand from that perch. And it is unrealistic to think that clergy will never need care from the people with whom they associate most—their parishioners. There is nothing emotionally or spiritually healthy about having unrealistic, unfair expectations of clergy. Each pastor has a distinctive personal history that likely includes some painful chapters. Each has strengths and weaknesses. Each has warts and personal foibles.

When wounded, pastors bleed. At the same time, congregations that drift into inappropriate caretaking of a seriously troubled pastor invite eventual damaging conflict. When a pastor has significant emotional problems, some parishioners may want to be protective—to shield the pastor from criticism or to cover up his or her inappropriate behavior. In this kind of situation, responsible lay leaders should summon appropriate denominational officials—a bishop, executive presbyter, district superintendent, or conference minister—those who are called to minister to pastors and to help congregations deal with these issues. That summons must be immediate if allegations of clergy sexual or financial misconduct arise.

PASTOR-PARISH RELATIONS COMMITTEES

Many congregations select a committee to deal with relations between clergy and parishioners. These committees are no panacea. Unless they function with integrity, they can be worse than nothing.

The underlying rationale for such committees is that pastors and parishioners need some discreet arena in which to voice concerns about each other, a setting where those concerns can be resolved without unduly embarrassing either clergy or congregation members. A pastor, for example, might be frustrated with trustees who refuse to pay for basic parsonage repairs or with a diaconate, vestry, or session that vetoes any suggested changes in the worship service. In a few cases, the pastor may need to vent some legitimate frustrations or even to acknowledge a significant personal problem and to seek advice or assistance. Parishioners might go to such a committee if they are dissatisfied with the response from another board or committee when they raised concerns about some aspect of the pastor's behavior. Perhaps the deacons have failed to respond when some parishioners think the minister is refusing to make certain pastoral calls or when his or her preaching is too political or personal for their taste.

Pastor-parish relations committees are effective only when committee members have the trust of *both* pastors and parishioners. If the trust of either is lacking, the pastor or parishioners will not feel safe expressing candid concerns. Too often, such a committee favors only the pastor or only complaining parishioners and in the process becomes ineffective or worse, destructive.

Dysfunctional pastor-parish relations committees can become an arena for unfair attacks on clergy. I served on one such committee and know of another that devoted serious consideration to allegations against pastors contained in unsigned letters. That was wrong and hurtful. The temptation to deal with anonymous complaints is strong. Committee members may worry that these complaints signal serious underlying congregational unrest, and they will be anxious to keep the peace. They may fear that if they ignore anonymous critics, those critics will leave the church. But responding to such complaints is toxic—not only to the target of the complaints, but to the entire congregation. God's justice demands that those voicing complaints be held accountable for what they allege. Dealing with anonymous complaints or improperly protecting the anonymity of complainants invites irresponsibility. If people know they can criticize without being identified, they may feel free to hurl all manner of untrue allegations at a minister or a lay leader simply because they harbor a personal dislike. By the same token, accepting anonymous complaints destroys the feeling of congregational safety and trust. After all, if a committee acts on anonymous complaints against the pastor or a lay leader, parishioners reasonably might fear that any one of them could become the next target.

These committees can also do harm if they shield clergy from being held accountable for their conduct or if they become a forum for pastors to voice "confidential" allegations about laypeople. Ultimately, this manner of protecting the minister will backfire and cause the minister more trouble. If committees fail to address appropriately stated concerns when they are first voiced and relatively easy resolution is possible, problems generally will mount to crisis levels at which they cannot be ignored or easily resolved.

IS THE PASTOR THE ISSUE?

There certainly are occasions when the pastor is *the* major relevant issue in congregational conflict. Clearly in cases of clergy sexual or financial misconduct, the pastor should be removed. There may be other situations in which the pastor and the congregation have grown in different directions and the relationship between them no longer works. More often, I suspect, the pastor becomes the lightning rod for conflict between and among congregational factions. In the pulpit each Sunday, the pastor is more visible more often than anyone else in the church. When parishioners disagree, the pastor, unfortunately, often takes the heat.

If half the congregation really appreciates the pastor's use of inclusive language and introduction of newer, inclusive hymns while the other half is furious about these changes, the issue is probably not the pastor. The issue is a sharp difference of opinion among parishioners. Criticizing the pastor will not resolve the issue. The issue requires thoughtful conversation among parishioners and exploration of how their differing spiritual needs and expectations might be addressed.

If half the congregation seeks justice-based preaching on issues of race, sexual orientation, and economic circumstance while the other half denounces such sermons as bringing politics into the pulpit, the issue is not the pastor. It is differing understandings of how the Gospel calls parishioners to be faithful. If half the congregation wants to raise funds for a new parish hall and the other half wants to raise money for mission outreach, the issue is not the pastor. It is differing approaches to stewardship among parishioners.

I suspect that issues such as these are often placed at the pastor's doorstep because parishioners are afraid to confront the reality that their own differing views are at the heart of the conflict. Congregations that struggle to meet budgets and maintain facilities fear that facing disagreements among parishioners will "split the church." It is easier and feels safer to blame the minister. However, congregations that repeatedly project their own internal disagreements on their minister are likely to experience a series of short-term pastorates, either dismissing clergy or receiving clergy resignations every two or three years. Meanwhile, the underlying disagreements remain.

When conflict seems to focus on the pastor, fit congregations will step back from the fray and consider what is really going on. If the conflict issues involve disagreements between parish factions, these congregations will open them up and deal with them. They may even call in outside assistance from denominational officials or consultants. They will keep good pastors and clear the air.

In summary, striking a healthy balance between pastoral authority and accountability is a fine art. It is best accomplished when communication is good and parishioners clearly understand the unique qualities of the clergy vocation. Pastor-parish relations committees may be helpful if they earn and enjoy the trust of both clergy and congregation and implement processes that hold all parties accountable. Fit congregations will not blame their own internal squabbles on the minister.

Questions for Reflection

1. How is pastoral authority recognized or ignored in your church?

2. To whom is your minister accountable on a regular basis?

3. What kinds of informal or formal discussions occur about your pastor's sermons? How do you understand "freedom of the pulpit"?

4. How is decision-making shared between your pastor and lay leaders?

5. How focused are you on the pastor? Is your pastor placed on a pedestal, or is your pastor blamed for everything that goes wrong? Are you able to discern which issues are disagreements between parishioners and which truly involve the pastor?

6. How do you care for your pastor? Do you provide adequate time for rest, vacation, and continuing education? How do you support your pastor when he or she must deal with personal issues such as illness or grief?

Chapter 11

WHEN YOU NEED HELP

Nothing seems to be working. Whenever we try to get the dea-cons and trustees together to work out their problems, the fighting just gets nastier. We need help!

All this disagreement is getting ugly, and people are getting hurt. Mary and Joe and several others have stopped coming to church because they say they no longer enjoy the atmo-sphere. What can we do?

I'm on the pastor-parish relations committee, and we've tried to get the church council and minister to sit down and work out their problems. But they've all dug their heels in and won't give an inch. And now others in the church are taking sides. I don't know what else we can do.

Up to this point, we have been exploring healthy processes and behav-ioral habits that promote congregational fitness. But just as athletes sometimes are injured and require the services of sports doctors, so congre-gations and individual parishioners sometimes become so injured or wounded that they need outside assistance to recover and return to a fit condition. The remainder of this book examines sound ways to seek and benefit from such assistance for both congregations and individuals.

When comments like the ones cited at the beginning of this chapter become frequent, it is probably time to seek outside help. There are times when emotions are running so high and the parties are so stuck in their respective positions that it is prudent to seek calmer, more objective assistance from one or more competent denominational officials or consultants. Congregations often are wary of calling in help from the outside. "We don't need anybody else; we can handle this ourselves," parishioners may say. But asking for help is not a sign of congregational failure. In fact, it is the wise congregation that recognizes the need for outside assistance before the battles turn bloody. After all, congregations—especially small to medium-size ones—often compare themselves to extended families. We need to remember that even loving families sometimes need family counseling.

Usually, the first step is to summon a judicatory official—someone from the conference, district, presbytery, or diocese. These are leaders charged with caring for congregations and pastors in their region or state. They may, after assessing the situation, seek to mediate the conflict themselves, or they may suggest retaining others with experience in this field.

WHO SHOULD MANAGE THE CONFLICT?

When the conflict manager dispatched to a conflicted church is a judicatory official—a bishop, general presbyter, superintendent, or conference minister—it is crucial to be clear about the role that person will play. Without such clarity, conflict-of-interest issues may arise, muddying an already complicated situation. For example, these officials sometimes function as pastors to parish clergy. It is to the bishop or superintendent or conference minister that clergy often turn when they need pastoral care. Clearly, clergy need such resources for their own emotional and spiritual health. And they may especially need such resources if they are under great stress as a result of conflict in the parish. But a denominational official who has been assigned and is carrying out the role of pastor to the church minister may understandably be perceived by laypeople—who are at odds with their minister—as one who will simply protect the minister. A similar perception may be applied to a denominational committee assigned to deal with such problems if that committee is dominated by clergy. "Oh, they're just like doctors and lawyers—they're going to cover up and protect their own" is a comment I have heard from laypeople. At the same time, an oversight committee dominated by laypeople may be perceived as having a bias against clergy.

This is not an attack on denominational officials or oversight committees. It is rather a statement of reality. In my former life as a newspaper reporter, I knew that the appearance of a conflict of interest could be just as damaging as a real one. In my own mind, I might be absolutely convinced that I could objectively report on a city council discussion of a proposed zoning-ordinance change. But if I signed a petition advocating that change, those who knew I had signed the petition would be suspicious of my reporting, no matter how objective my articles were. Their understandable suspicion, in turn, would make my reporting less credible. Similarly, the appearance of a possible conflict of interest on the part of a denominational official summoned to help resolve a conflict can throw the entire process out of kilter. Increasingly, where finances permit, churches and judicatories are turning to professional outside mediators or conflict managers.

But many churches and many regional denominational bodies lack the funds to hire outside resources or, if they have the funds, are reluctant to pay for outside assistance. Some, then, turn to another option—trained clergy from other churches in the denomination. That makes good sense if and only if, the clergy have been properly trained, have some sound conflict-management experience, and bring along no personal emotional baggage. If pastors are stressed by conflict in their own churches, they may bring their frustration, anxiety, and even anger to your situation. Incompetent or emotionally impaired conflict managers can wreak great damage on an already hurting church. If a congregation has a bad experience with an outside resource, either a denominational official or a consultant, it will be reluctant to seek outside help again.

Thus, it is incumbent upon denominational officials that they dispatch conflict managers who:

1. Have no appearance of role conflict.

2. Have received relevant training and acquired some experience, perhaps interning with more experienced managers.

3. Do not come into a conflicted church with their own agenda or with latent anger, guilt, or any other unhealthy emotional baggage stemming from their own parish situation. This applies to lay consultants as well as to ordained clergy.

CHOOSING A CONSULTANT

There are no licensing or credentialing requirements for church consultants. Just about anyone can hang out a shingle or print up some business cards and attempt to enter this field. I know because I sought in vain for some prescribed set of hoops through which I should jump before offering my own services as a congregational studies consultant. So how can lay leaders find and retain competent consultants?

1. Obviously, you will want to examine a person's training. There are some certificate programs in conflict management. The Alban Institute offers courses in this area, as do various seminaries and divinity schools. Mediation training is offered by various universities and professional associations.

2. Even more important, check references. Talk with clergy and lay leaders in churches where this consultant has worked. Successful work with other churches is far more important than academic degrees. Years of training mean little if the consultant lacks the personal skills necessary to work with parishioners and clergy who are likely to be anxious, frustrated, and even angry in the middle of a conflicted situation.

3. Seek an initial face-to-face interview with a consultant candidate to get a feel for his or her style and approach.

4. Once you believe you have found the right person, develop a written agreement that discusses the approach, the amount of time you jointly anticipate this effort will require, the cost, and the method of payment. Consultants often seek one-third of their fee at the beginning, one-third midway through the process, and the final third at the conclusion of the work.

WHAT TO EXPECT

1. *Do not expect a quick fix.* Certainly, if the conflict involves serious allegations of clergy or parishioner wrongdoing such as sexual or financial misconduct, the alleged wrongdoer should be immediately separated from access to potential victims or funds. This should be done without prejudice. That is, it should be clear that this separation is not a judgment of guilt but is implemented until the issues can be examined and a determination of guilt or innocence can be made. At the same time, some cases involving alleged sexual or financial misconduct require immediate involvement by legal or law-enforcement authorities. Judicatory officials or consultants cannot and should not attempt to supplant the legal process when a crime is alleged. Congregations place themselves in legal jeopardy if they fail to take appropriate action in such cases. But even in these cases—perhaps especially in these cases—the work required to resolve the congregational conflict will take time and significant effort.

As noted earlier, healthy resolution of conflict that leads to reconciliation requires carefully "unpacking" of what has happened. And "what has happened" likely will include not only what doctors call the "presenting symptoms" (such as a dispute between the pastor and some parishioners or between two boards or two congregational factions), but also what has happened over years, even decades. If a significant part of the problem involves habitual and deeply ingrained dysfunctional congregational processes or behaviors, it will take time to understand their origins and to develop healthier alternatives. Parishioners already physically and emotionally worn out by the conflict may find this time requirement difficult to accept. But shortcuts seldom are effective and long lasting.

2. *Do not expect the consultant to "fix" things.* Only you, the members of the congregation, can make the necessary repairs in processes and relationships. I became keenly aware of this unrealistic expectation when I first met with a church council to discuss conducting a congregational study. I expected resistance because, I had been told, the people in this church were exhausted and near burnout. Instead, I was warmly welcomed by council members because they hoped I could fix their situation. I quickly corrected their assumption. I said I could provide them with information and perspectives, and could put what they probably already knew into some coherent form that might help them make informed decisions about their future. But, I emphasized, those decisions must be theirs.

3. *Expect to do some hard, even painful work.* By the time a conflict has reached the point at which outside help is needed, it is usually complicated. A tangled cycle of recriminations and defensive responses may have developed. Chances are that no single person or group of persons must or should shoulder all the blame. The most effective resolutions of conflict often are achieved ultimately in an atmosphere of mutual repentance.

4. *Expect to develop and be asked to follow some guidelines for the conduct of conflict-management sessions.* These sessions should not be verbal free-for-alls. You likely will be asked to listen respectfully to each other, not to interrupt, to refrain from labeling or name-calling, and to speak only for yourself and not for unnamed others. Expect to be held to "fair fight" standards.

5. *Expect to learn or refresh some relational skills.* For example, a manager may take you through some exercises in active listening and ask you to "echo back" what the previous person has said before you make your point.

6. *Expect that the conflict manager will respect your unique situation.* Be wary of and resist any quick attempt by the manager to apply some generalized pattern to your situation—to insist that your problems fit a standard, inflexible model. While some dysfunctional congregational behaviors can be observed in a number of churches, each congregation is unique, with its own collection of unique individuals and relationships.

MANAGING THE IN-BETWEEN TIMES

Now you have retained a conflict-management consultant and set up a schedule of meetings. These sessions may extend over several months. How do you function in the meantime? Unless some thought is given to this issue, there is a good chance that the conflict will be exacerbated. Any conflict resolution process has a better chance of succeeding with the least permanent damage if the issues can remain clear and uncluttered by whatever happens between meetings and if emotions are not further inflamed between those sessions.

But few church conflicts are resolved overnight. Instead, they often lead to a series of meetings, which may be separated by weeks if not months. In the meantime, weekly worship services must be planned, bills must be paid and contributions recorded, attention must be paid to people who need visits from the pastor or a lay leader, Sunday school classes and youth-group gatherings may continue, church suppers and fairs may need to be planned and conducted, and food cupboards may need to be staffed—to name just a few "housekeeping tasks." Many of them require communication between pastor and lay leaders or between committees and boards. If relationships between or among these parties already are strained by the conflict, these folk may continue to rub each other raw while trying to handle these day-to-day responsibilities.

It may be prudent then, at the very beginning of any conflict-management session, to recognize this danger and, if possible, to establish procedures that minimize the risk of making matters worse. Perhaps during this period necessary communication between a board and pastor or between two boards or committees can be delegated to lay leaders who are the least emotionally involved. It may even make sense to postpone some discretionary events such as church suppers. Each congregation will have different needs and different ways of working out these necessary ongoing activities in ways that minimize worsening the conflict. This need for laypeople to continue carrying out their responsibilities in the midst of a conflicted situation is one, I have discovered, that ordained clergy sometimes fail to recognize. You might not even think about it until you have to plan for monthly communion with the pastor from whom you are estranged, or to coordinate worship planning by the vestry, session, or diaconate, and the music committee or choir director when those relationships are involved in the conflict. For this reason, I suggest that you seek the counsel and leadership of the conflict manager at the very beginning of the management process to work out careful "in-between" guidelines.

If the conflict is between the congregation (or a significant segment of the congregation) and the pastor, provisions should be made for interim pastoral care for those estranged from the pastor. Otherwise, parishioners who suffer illness, the death of a loved one, or some other serious personal crisis during the conflict-management process will be left without caring counsel and, as a result, become even more frustrated and angry.

Even those who do not have an immediate crisis, especially the elderly, may feel frightened by estrangement from the pastor. One older parishioner put it this way: "If I become seriously ill, who will come and pray with me, hear my doubts and fears, and comfort me? And if I die, who will conduct my funeral?" If older members are not reassured that some interim pastoral care will be available, they may leave the church with which they have been intimately connected for decades, even a lifetime, for the church down the street that seems peaceful and whose pastor seems to be well liked.

This situation—this need for interim pastoral care—can pose an especially difficult ethical dilemma for parishioners who are estranged from their pastor. They may understandably feel uncomfortable seeking pastoral care from another local minister or from another pastor in their denomination, not wanting to expose their church's problems to others. Even if they are displeased with their pastor, they still may not want to embarrass her by going elsewhere for pastoral counsel.

In an ideal situation, the pastor in question will recognize this need and be prepared to refer parishioners to one or more clergy who agree to provide this service. If that scenario is not in place, lay leaders should ask denominational officials to make provisions for temporary, alternative pastoral care. It also makes sense that some uninvolved clergy be available for those laypeople wounded by the conflict. Clergy may be wary of providing such assistance for fear they will be inappropriately drawn into the problems. But wounded laypeople with no pastoral-care resources are, again, likely to become more and more frustrated. With wise pastoral counsel, they may be much better prepared to enter into a healthy resolution process.

A clergywoman friend suggested that retired and experienced intentional interim ministers might provide temporary pastoral services to both wounded layfolk and stressed pastors. This makes a great deal of sense. With their training and experience, these clergy would be prepared to deal with the emotions and pain associated with congregational conflict. Moreover, because they are retired, they could easily isolate that assignment of temporary pastor to a few parishioners without risking any role confusion. In fact, I would encourage lay leaders to lobby their denominational bodies to develop a cadre of pastors who are available to serve in this capacity.

One final caveat regarding the in-between time. All parties—laypeople and clergy—should be attentive to the conflict-management process. If it appears that the consultants or denominational officials are not exercising good judgment and are making matters worse, do not be afraid to call for a temporary halt and consider seeking replacements. This can be a tough call. What may seem to be unproductive and even damaging conflict-management techniques may simply be the hard, sometimes painful processes required to work through a complicated situation. On the other hand, if parties feel they or others are being shamed, scapegoated, or otherwise treated unfairly, they should name those feelings. Pastors and lay leaders should not be reluctant to call a halt to processes that they think are unjust, personally demeaning, or otherwise destructive. However, they then should seek alternative outside assistance. Aborting a conflict-resolution process, with no follow-up, solves nothing. In fact, chances are that problems may seem worse and wounds may be deeper at this juncture since allegations and emotional outbursts usually surface during early rounds of the resolution process. Left untreated, those allegations and outbursts will only push the conflict to a more serious level at which a win-win resolution may become impossible.

HEALTHY SOLUTIONS

As I have mentioned in earlier chapters, conflict can trigger a variety of emotions and behaviors that may seem almost automatic—anger, fear, anxiety, denial, avoidance, taking sides, "herding up," careless listening, fighting, or fleeing. Taken together, they almost guarantee a win-lose or lose-lose outcome. I suspect the latter is more often the result, although winners may not recognize at first what they and their church have lost. Win-lose resolutions usually mean that some parishioners will leave. Some losers may remain, determined to win the next battle. Winners may be left with unspoken but very real guilt feelings. And win-lose endings often leave in their wake a continuing unsettled atmosphere that does not feel fully safe to those who remain.

Fit congregations have trained themselves to counter all these unhealthy emotions and behaviors with healthy ones. They will have learned to work through their fear or to give it over to God, to ease their anxieties by living and loving the questions at hand, to listen thoughtfully, and to acknowledge problems and responsibly participate in a fair resolution process. Congregations intent on win-win resolutions will be more creative in exploring options. Their parishioners are more likely to think and speak with clarity, to take their stands while respecting those with whom they disagree. They will care when fellow parishioners are hurting. They will keep living and loving the questions about how God may be speaking to them at this time.

Developing a healthy solution depends on two steps: accurately defining the problem, dispute or conflict; and committing to a healthy process for working out the solution. In fact, the congregation's overall well-being and faithful witness may hinge more on the process than the result.

Much of this book has been devoted to unpacking issues, because that is the process required to get to the real problem, to define it accurately. Too often, for example, the "problem" may initially and reactively be defined as the pastor, although the real conflict concerns two or more congregational factions or a matter of poor communication or simply habitually dysfunctional congregational behavior. So it is important to take the time and do the work required to name the real problem.

Remember that what is most important to faithful bystanders may not be the solution but the process employed to find it. Pushing for a speedy apparent resolution that scapegoats the pastor or some parishioners, that unnecessarily puts some people down, is a flawed process that will leave in its wake a wounded congregation. Just as covering a major wound with a Band-Aid only postpones the necessary treatment or surgery, declaring resolution when all that has been achieved is a temporary and tenuous truce only postpones and may even inflame congregational conflict. That is why what seem to be win-lose solutions too often end up with everybody losing.

This is not to say that every conflict can be resolved without pain or loss. Sometimes a pastor and congregation simply are not a good match. Sometimes, despite the best and most prayerful efforts, laypeople or, occasionally, clergy continue to behave so destructively that conflict resolution must firmly put an end to that behavior within the church, even if that means dismissing a pastor or recalling one or more lay officers. But fit congregations will not jump to resolutions that force people out. Instead, they will see that path as a last resort when all else fails. Beginning and staying with a focus on developing win-win solutions to problems makes it much more likely that win-win resolutions can be achieved.

Questions for Reflection

1. What role do your state or regional denominational officials play in caring for congregations and pastors? If your congregation required outside help, to whom would you turn?

2. What are your expectations of outside consultants? How do they agree with or differ from the expectations described in this chapter?

3. What are some other potential "in-between times" issues you might want to address? What ongoing congregational activities might feel the impact of conflict and the resolution process?

4. Think of some problems your congregation has confronted and how they were resolved. List them under "Win-Win," "Win-Lose," and "Lose-Lose" columns. Discuss the differences in process and outcome. How were win-win resolutions achieved? What were the consequences of win-lose resolutions?

Chapter 12

IF YOU ARE WOUNDED

I've never been so hurt. I gave all those years to the church, teaching Sunday school, making pies for bake sales, cooking for church suppers. Now, because I voiced my opinion about spending so much money on the church building, half the congregation isn't speaking to me.

I don't know what to believe anymore. I've always trusted ministers, but Reverend Clark outright lied about the senior warden. I guess he's threatened by strong lay leaders. But now, how can I believe anything the minister says from the pulpit?

I have to wonder if God is anywhere near this church, the way people treat each other. They crucified the pastor when she was only doing her job. I'm afraid churches are all alike— just a bunch of hypocrites. But now whom can I rely on?

Being in the center or even on the fringes of a serious congregational conflict can be very painful. We may feel blindsided. This kind of thing is not supposed to happen in a church! Taken by surprise, we are not prepared for the rush of emotions that floods us. We are hurt, angry, confused, feeling guilty or self-righteous or a combination of both. We want to strike out or we want to hide away, depending on the moment. We may feel betrayed by friends. Here are folk with whom we worshiped Sunday after Sunday, with whom we washed dishes in the church kitchen, or planted shrubs on the church lawn, people whose woes we patiently heard, friends for whom we cooked or baby-sat when there was illness in their families.

Now they shun us or act as if nothing has happened. When we try to talk about our concerns, they turn us off or turn away. We may feel betrayed by the pastor, even by God. Where is God, we ask, in the midst of all this ugliness?

That Helpless Feeling

We may feel helpless. We cannot imagine remaining in the middle of this mess, especially if we think we are unfairly under attack. At the same time, we have devoted ten, 20, 30, or 40 years to this church, and we cannot imagine worshipping anywhere else. Leaving would be like walking away from our family. And if we start attending the church down the street, everybody there will know something is wrong. Maybe they will be leery of us because they have heard that we were involved in a church fight and they are afraid we are going to bring our anger and frustration to their church. Or maybe they will pressure us to jump ship prematurely and transfer our membership to their congregation.

There may be times when a church conflict is so serious, so personally painful, and so unlikely to be resolved in an acceptable way that leaving is the healthiest thing to do. More often, staying and trying to be part of the solution is the more faithful option. But how can we be part of the solution when we are so confused, upset, and hurt? What can we do? Consider the advice of business executive Frank Martin to "retreat and regroup." In his book *War in the Pews: A Foxhole Guide to Surviving Church Conflict*, he talks about his own experience.

> Weighed down with the stress of conflict, we decided to back away from our involvement and try to sort out the situation. . . before we could even think clearly about the issues, we needed to slow down our motors and retreat.[1]

Regrouping is not so easy. It is one of those strange dichotomies of life that at the very time when we most want to crawl away to nurse our pain and sorrow, we may need to be the most assertive, taking the initiative. We need to be faithful in caring for our wounded souls. Unless we have sought professional counseling in the past, most of us expect to find that type of care in our church. When that source for our soul care is temporarily unavailable, we are likely to feel lost and helpless. However, there are alternatives that will provide much-needed perspective and renewed spiritual strength. Retreating and regrouping should not be merely a time to lick wounds. It should be a time of self-examination as well. Temporarily withdrawing from the battlefront may decrease our own defensiveness about whatever mistakes we have made as well as decrease our anger about those whom we believe have hurt us. We can step back from the fray, learn more about ourselves, nourish a richer relationship with God, and then be better prepared to be part of the solution to our congregational turmoil.

STEPS TO HEALING

Here are five steps I took when I realized I needed some self-care:

1. Find a Pastoral Counselor

The purpose here is not to find someone to take your "side" in the conflict, but to help you sort out your emotions, feelings, and values, to help you connect with and experience God. When I did this, I asked a simple question of myself—"What does it mean for me to be faithful in this situation?"—and asked the pastor to help me find the answer. Note that I said I asked him to "help me find the answer." I did not ask him to "give me the answer." I met with him eight or ten times over the course of a year, sharing my struggle with this question. Mostly, he listened. That was incredibly important. When we have been involved in a serious, even destructive conflict, many voices are raised at once. We are usually so bent on mentally preparing our next statement, argument, or defense that we seldom really hear what others are saying and, by the same token, we seldom feel that we have been heard. And when we are in the midst of a battle, we are not likely to expose our vulnerabilities and uncertainties. Being able to open up with an experienced listener is an important first step to healing.

Occasionally, my pastoral counselor asked some gentle questions to help me clarify my thoughts and feelings. He passed on several essays and articles that had a similar effect. I remember one in particular, about a man working through his own "dark night of the soul." It was comforting to read how someone else weathered that experience, to realize that it is this experience that often leads to deeper spiritual development and a closer connection with God.

The challenge is finding an appropriate pastoral counselor. First, let me suggest how *not* to do this. It is tempting simply to go down the street or across town to talk to a minister in another local church or to another pastor in your denomination. Doing either places that other pastor in a difficult ethical bind, however, because he or she probably has some working relationship with your pastor—in a local ministerium or other ecumenical group or in denominational circles. Those who can afford to pay a professional may choose from telephone or other directory listings of pastoral counselors or seek a counselor recommended by a friend. Another option is to ask a denominational official for suggestions. There may be retired clergy nearby who could provide this service at minimal or no cost and without the ethical concerns facing active clergy. I was able to connect with a local retired clergyman of a denomination other than my own. He had no ongoing contact with the pastor of my church either in the local ministerium or in denominational circles.

2. Read and Reflect

Consider the term "retreat" in its spiritual sense, as a period of meditation rather than simply as a withdrawal from the battlefront. The simple act of sitting quietly in solitude with a book has a calming effect. We step away from the conflict to gain some distance, and we engage in some thoughtful contemplation. Turn to Scripture, perhaps with a study aid that will guide your reflections. Look for appropriate books or periodicals in your local bookstore or seminary library, or on-line. A variety of helpful reading materials is available. I would suggest first seeking material for spiritual reflection. The works of Dutch-born priest Henri Nouwen, who examined so many dimensions of the soul and spirituality, may be especially helpful, for he, too, experienced dark nights of the soul and wrote eloquently about those experiences and how they drew him closer to God. Periodicals such as *Weavings*,[2] a bi-monthly magazine of essays addressing various spiritual issues, provide thoughtful soul nourishment. The writings of poet and author Kathleen Norris—*Dakota: A Spiritual Geography, Amazing Grace: a Vocabulary of Faith*, and *The Cloister Walk*—are other excellent choices, not only for their content, but for the author's style, which conveys a sense of serenity even amid confusion and struggle. The blessing of these works is that they can be read slowly and deliberately, and they invite frequent pauses for reflection. Ultimately, you may find it helpful to read a few books on church conflict, on healthy ways to deal with it, and on how others have coped with it. The bibliography includes a number of books on congregational dynamics and conflict.

3. Pray

This retreat time can be an opportunity to grow in prayer—to move from "official" prayer language, which we often think is required, to simple, heart-felt conversations with God. In prayer, we can express our anger, our frustration, our guilt—whatever our emotions may be—in everyday language. One exercise frequently suggested by spiritual directors is to pray the Psalms. When we think of the Psalms, we tend to think mostly of the pastoral ones such as the 23rd Psalm or those that praise God, such as Psalm 100. But overall, the Psalms are pretty accurate scriptural representations of our humanity. The psalmists often rail at God, vent their anger and pain, even call down vengeance on their perceived enemies. But always they return to affirm God's steadfast love, care, and protection. Eugene Peterson's psalm paraphrases in his book *The Message* may be especially useful in this regard. They speak in language with which we all can identify. Here is how Peterson—poet, writer, and spiritual theology professor emeritus—paraphrases the beginning of Psalm 56:

> Take my side, God—I'm getting kicked around,
>   stomped on every day.
> Not a day goes by
>   but somebody beats me up.
> They make it their duty
>   to beat me up.
> When I get really afraid
>   I come to you in trust.
> I'm proud to praise God;
>   fearless now, I trust in God
> What can mere mortals do?[3]

Or the beginning of Psalm 77:

> I yell out to my God, I yell with all my might.
> I yell at the top of my lungs. He listens.
> I found myself in trouble and went looking for my Lord;
> my life was an open wound that wouldn't heal.[4]

Like the psalmists, we may need first to vent our frustrations, even if we may later sense we were wallowing too deeply in self-pity and self-righteousness. Then practice prayer as listening to God. Too often we think of prayer as one-way communication—we talk to God—and we forget to listen for God speaking to us. I suppose that we mostly drown God out in our fervent pleas and cut God off in our hasty "amens." I found help in verses of Psalm 139:

> Oh LORD, you have searched me and known me.
> You know when I sit down and when I rise up.
>   you discern my thoughts from far away.
> You search out my path and my lying down,
>   and are acquainted with all my ways.
> Even before a word is on my tongue,
>   O LORD, you know it completely.
>   . . . .
> Search me, O God, and know my heart;
>   test me and know my thoughts.
> See if there is any wicked way in me,
>   and lead me in the way everlasting. (Psalm 139:1-4, 23-24)

I found this psalm comforting when I was so confused that I could not even utter an articulate plea to God. So I prayed something like this: "God, you know my thoughts before I say them. Tonight I cannot even speak them because I am so confused." I simply lifted up that confusion and frustration to God and then tried to listen, to simply be quiet and wait. Sometimes in those moments, I heard something like an answer. But sometimes it was enough just to feel that God did indeed know my inner turmoil and that God would lighten my load by carrying my burden. And when I had been wallowing in self-righteousness, praying this psalm or my own paraphrase pulled me back on track, especially as I asked God to search me, test me, know my thoughts, and then lead me back to a faithful path.

There may be few occasions when engaging in this kind of conversation with God is as difficult and yet as crucial as those times when we have been wounded, confused, or frustrated by what is going on in our congregation. There may be no place in our lives other than our faith community where we expect so much from ourselves and from each other and feel so bereft when that community fails to meet our expectations. Some people may complain that I should have made prayer the number-one priority in this list of suggested self-care activities. I purposely listed it after seeking some counsel and doing some reading and reflection because I believe those activities can nourish and enrich prayer experience. A gentle question from a counselor or a particularly thought-provoking book passage can lead to new avenues of prayer.

4. Seek Study Opportunities

Take advantage of opportunities for Bible study unconnected to your church. If a theological seminary is nearby, consider auditing a course. Perhaps a nearby church or even a bookstore is conducting a spiritually oriented study. Sign up.

Almost by coincidence, as the conflict in my own church grew, a friend suggested I audit a course on "Approaching Ministry" at Bangor Theological Seminary. Fortunately, the professor approached the subject from the perspective of lay as well as ordained ministry. Initially, I listened carefully to try to understand what might be going on for my pastor. But soon I got caught up in examining my own ministry as a layperson. What was I called to be and do? Writing the papers for this course helped me think through some key personal issues. The following semester, I enrolled in a seminary course on spiritual identity, which proved to be enormously helpful. Rather than focusing on those I believed had hurt me, I began to explore my own relationship with God and gained, I hope, an even clearer sense of who God was calling me to be. At the same time, this course helped me better understand those with whom I was at odds, and as my understanding increased, my anger, frustration, and pain ebbed.

5. Find a Resting Place

Sometimes, even in the most difficult and painful conflict, we can stay the course. We can continue worshipping with our faith community while praying for and, with God's grace, participating in healing. But sometimes we need to draw apart physically for a while, just as Christ sometimes did.

Several people have told me that they were so angry, hurt, and frustrated by the conflict in their congregations that they no longer found any comfort or nourishment worshipping there. In fact, Sunday mornings were torture. They arrived at the church doors braced for snubs or angry glares, spent some of the worship time tallying who was present and who was absent and much of the rest nursing their wounds or mentally rehearsing what they would like to say to those with whom they disagreed. They avoided coffee fellowship and went home feeling guilty.

When attending worship or participating in activities in your church becomes this stressful, it may be time to take a sabbatical. It may be time to find, for a while, a place apart where you can be spiritually fed and even restored by worship. Again, this move may feel uncomfortable. If you live in a relatively small community and begin attending worship at a nearby church, your presence probably will signal to others that something is amiss in your own congregation. Chances are, in a small community, these folk already will have heard talk about those troubles. They may want to pump you for details. They may be wary, fearing that you will bring your problems to them. Or they may immediately invite you to join their congregation.

When it seemed prudent for me to absent myself for a while from my own church, I was fortunate to find none of these responses at a church barely a block away. Instead, I found people who were warm and welcoming without being intrusive or pressuring. Perhaps that was because that congregation had weathered its own storm some years before, and several of its members had temporarily worshipped with my congregation. They appreciated the value of sanctuary—of having a place to go to be nourished until it was safe to return to their own church. Several months after I began attending the neighboring church, I asked to talk with the pastor. I explained that I would probably never join his church, since it was a different denomination from my own, but that I needed to be away from my own for a while. I even said that if I concluded that I could no longer be a part of my home congregation, I would probably migrate to another one of my denomination some 30 miles away, so strong were my ties to that tradition. That pastor was understanding. "I hear what you're saying. Just consider our church a resting place," he said. What a wonderful term—a resting place. That was what I needed—rest from the conflict, truly a place to retreat and regroup. Those not fortunate enough to have such an understanding church nearby might consider simply visiting a number of churches a little farther away from home for a few months. In this way, it is unlikely that pastors or parishioners will have unrealistic expectations or undue concerns regarding your presence.

When we engage in several, if not all, of these activities, we may experience a kind of spiritual and emotional rebirth. Where once we were hurting, confused, angry, and even feeling disconnected from God, we will have gained some distance and perspective and developed a closer relationship with God. Although time does not necessarily heal all wounds, it gradually diminishes the pain. If we have sought some guidance, read and reflected, learned new ways of prayer, and found some temporary nourishing worship, we are apt to be stronger, more spiritually and emotionally centered, perhaps even ready to return to our own faith community with a fresh outlook.

Separate but Connected

A key benefit of such a self-care regimen is its potential to help us function more effectively in a conflicted congregational situation. We face two competing realities when we have been wounded by church conflict:

1. When we are hurt, we understandably tend to huddle together with other wounded souls as we nurse and seek healing for those wounds. We crave and need support from others who have had a similar experience and understand what we're going through. We ache for "togetherness."

2. At the same time, no two of us were wounded in exactly the same way, and none of us reacts in exactly the same way to whatever happened. Rather, each of us reacts out of unique life experiences, personalities, and emotional states. One may be consumed with anger, another with guilt, another pensive and experiencing that dark night of the soul. We also heal at different rates. The temptation is either to hunker down with others and ignore our unique reactions and feelings, or to play Lone Ranger. Increasingly, family-systems theorists suggest a third alternative—differentiation. That term describes an emotionally healthy state of being clear about who you are, about your unique self, values, thoughts, instincts, and judgments, separate from pressure for togetherness with others while still remaining connected with those others. It means being able calmly to assert your views and understandings without cutting yourself off from those who hold

opposing views. For me, it meant being able to give and receive support from a group of friends while separating out my own reactions and thoughts and charting my own future course.

Differentiation receives extensive treatment in a number of books.[5] For purposes here, consider how Ronald W. Richardson, a pastoral counselor and systems theorist, defines the term in his book *Creating a Healthier Church*. Differentiation is wisdom—a "people's ability to effectively use what they know," he says, requiring "a lower level of chronic anxiety and a greater ability to think clearly in anxious situations."[6]

Retreating and regrouping can significantly increase our differentiation quotient. We can get a clearer fix on who we are individually when we take time to talk things out with a pastoral counselor, read and reflect, develop a closer connection with God through prayer, perhaps participate in a study group, and maybe even remove ourselves temporarily from worshipping in our home church. That is how we separate. We connect when we return to the congregational fold that may still be troubled. Calmer, less anxious, and more grounded in our own identity, we are better prepared to participate in the congregational healing, messy as it may be, without feeling unduly threatened.

Questions for Reflection

1. Have you ever been wounded by a conflict in a church? How did that feel? What were your immediate reactions? What did you do?

2. What resources are available for healing in your community? Do you have any ecumenical Bible study or spirituality groups? Does your church maintain a library of spiritually nourishing material that might be helpful?

3. What might it mean to be "separate but connected"? How might that work in your congregational situation?

4. How have you dealt with a significant personal upset—at work, in your family, in your neighborhood? How did you deal with your anger, frustration, and anxiety? Looking back, how might you have better handled that?

Chapter 13

THE REWARDS OF FITNESS

When we train in a gym, we build up muscle and flexibility. As a result, we have confidence that we can lift certain weights, vault certain heights, or run certain distances without suffering serious injury. When congregations develop healthy relational and procedural habits as a result of training, they build up confidence that they can handle problems, disagreements, and even conflicts without suffering serious injury to the church as a whole or to individual parishioners. Other practices—observing the no-talk rule, staying in denial, and when a crisis forces conflict into the open, pushing for premature closure—result in congregations' never experiencing the level of successful conflict resolution that reassures them they can do it again.

Learning how to handle conflict in a healthy manner is a bit like learning to ride a bicycle. The first time you set off on a two-wheeler, you may fall off and scrape your knees. But you get back on. Once you have tackled that task—managed to stay upright for a few blocks on smooth pavement, you gain the confidence to try it yet again. You know you can do that. You also may have gained enough confidence to do more—ride for several miles or tackle mountain biking on rougher trails. But for those who never got back on, bicycle riding looms as a threat rather than as a challenge.

In the same way, congregations that practice denial and premature closure tend to view every problem—even a minor one—as a threat. And, sure enough, when suppressed conflicts finally erupt in crisis in a congregation, the battle can be exceedingly destructive to individuals and the gathered community. Congregations that have worked through disagreements learn that they can tackle problems, even thorny ones, without long-term harm. When the next problem arises, they have some confidence that they can handle it. As that confidence builds, they have less anxiety about tackling tougher problems—divisive disputes over a social or theological issue or major misconduct on the part of a clergy or lay leader. Further, with less initial anxiety, congregations are likely to be successful handling those tougher issues.

Donald E. Bossart, a United Methodist minister and a retired professor of Iliff School of Theology, Denver, where he specialized in conflict resolution and interpersonal ministry courses, attests that the benefits of congregational fitness training are evident when parishioners confront even the most controversial issues. In the chapter he wrote for *Congregations Talking about Homosexuality: Dialogue on a Difficult Issue*, Bossart observes that the major learning that seemed to emerge from the book's congregational case studies is that "it is worthwhile to engage in constructive conflict rather than exist in harmonious dishonesty." He goes on to emphasize the rewards of such engagement:

> There are skills to be learned for dealing with conflict constructively, and these need to be a part of lay and pastoral leadership training for each congregation. The more experience a congregation has successfully addressing conflict, the better able members will be to create win/win scenarios even when dealing with topics as potentially divisive as homosexuality. The benefits of having dealt with any issues successfully and having come to know other members more deeply in the process builds and strengthens the community. . . . We no longer view difficult issues as roadblocks to effective ministry. Rather, we are inspired by these issues to be self-aware and clear in our communication.[1]

One final word. Although this book addresses ways in which congregations can develop fitness for successful conflict management, we should never assume that we are alone in the effort. We are in partnership with God. We need constantly to ask what God is doing in our midst—yes, even in the midst of a messy disagreement. Is God calling us to new growth? Is God calling us to set aside old grudges? Is God calling us to take a firm but respectful stand for God's justice, peace, and concern for the hurting and marginalized? Is God calling us to ease our grip on our own views so that we might genuinely hear others? Are we really open to the mystery of the Holy Spirit moving among us and calling us to speak the truth with love?

Notes

Introduction

1. Interim pastors serve congregations between the time one pastor leaves and the next settled pastor arrives. Increasingly, some clergy are being trained as "intentional interims," charged to help parishioners address congregational problems so they will be ready to proceed in a healthy manner when their new settled pastor arrives. "Afterpastors" generally are clergy who succeed pastors who have engaged in sexual misconduct with members of the congregation. However, I think the term can be applied as well to clergy called to congregations that have experienced destructive conflict that significantly wounded some parishioners—conflict that may not have been fully resolved.

Chapter 1. Why We Fight

1. Hugh F. Halverstadt, *Managing Church Conflict* (Louisville: Westminster John Knox, 1991), 2.

2. G. Lloyd Rediger, *Clergy Killers: Guidance for Pastors and Congregations Under Attack* (Minneapolis: Logos, 1997), 8.

3. Rediger, *Clergy Killers*, 101-109.

4. Halverstadt, *Managing Church Conflict*, 29-31.

Chapter 2. Conflict: Normal and Healthy or Destructive?

1. William H. Willimon, *Preaching about Conflict in the Local Church* (Philadelphia: Westminster, 1987), 50. Quotations used by permission of Westminster John Knox.

2. Willimon, *Preaching about Conflict*, 19.

3. Speed Leas, *Moving Your Church Through Conflict* (Washington, D.C.: Alban Institute, 1985), 27.

4. Rediger, *Clergy Killers*, 54.

5. Leas, *Moving Your Church Through Conflict*, 19.

6. Leas, *Moving Your Church Through Conflict*, 19-22.

Chapter 3. Who Are We and Why Are We Here?

1. Roy M. Oswald and Speed B. Leas, *The Inviting Church: A Study of New Member Assimilation* (Bethesda: Alban Institute, 1987), 8.

2. William H. Gregory, *Faith Before Faithfulness: Centering the Inclusive Church* (Cleveland: Pilgrim Press, 1992), 50-55.

3. Lyle E. Schaller, *The Interventionist* (Nashville: Abingdon, 1997), 127-137.

Chapter 4. Responsibility and Accountability

1. Halverstadt, *Managing Church Conflict*, 47.

2. Halverstadt, *Managing Church Conflict*, 47.

3. Halverstadt, *Managing Church Conflict*, 47.

4. Deborah Tannen, *The Argument Culture: Moving from Debate to Dialogue* (New York: Random House, 1998), 19-20.

5. Tannen, *Argument Culture*, 37.

6. Tannen, *Argument Culture*, 41-45.

Chapter 5. Reducing Anxiety

1. Joseph Phelps, *More Light, Less Heat: How Dialogue Can Transform Christian Conflicts Into Growth* (San Francisco: Jossey-Bass, 1999), 25.

2. M. Scott Peck, *Golf and the Spirit: Lessons for the Journey* (New York: Harmony Books, 1999), 67.

3. Rainer Maria Rilke, *Letters to a Young Poet* (New York: Vintage, 1986), 34.

Chapter 6. Repeal the No-Talk Rule

1. Speed Leas and Paul Kittlaus, *Church Fights: Managing Conflict in the Local Church* (Philadelphia: Westminster, 1973), 47. Quotations used by permission of Westminster John Knox.

2. Kenneth A. Halstead, *From Stuck to Unstuck: Overcoming Congregational Impasse* (Bethesda: Alban Institute, 1998), 79.

3. Nancy Myer Hopkins and Mark Laaser, eds., *Restoring the Soul of a Church: Healing Congregations Wounded by Clergy Sexual Misconduct* (Bethesda: Alban Institute, 1995), 249-250.

4. Kenneth Alan Moe. *The Pastor's Survival Manual: Ten Perils in Parish Ministry and How to Handle Them* (Bethesda: Alban Institute, 1995), 74-75.

Chapter 7. Beware of Platitudes

1. Halstead, *From Stuck to Unstuck*, 86-87.
2. Halstead, *From Stuck to Unstuck*, 80-81.
3. Halstead, *From Stuck to Unstuck*, 79.
4. Ellen Goodman, "Hurrying Healing," *Boston Globe*, January 4, 1998.

Chapter 8. Clear the Decks

1. Peterson, Eugene H., *Working the Angles: The Shape of Pastoral Integrity* (Grand Rapids: Eerdmans, 1987), 23.
2. For a more thorough description of this process, see Roy M. Oswald and Robert E. Friedrich, Jr., *Discerning Your Congregation's Future: A Strategic and Spiritual Approach* (Bethesda: Alban Institute, 1996), 64-75.

Chapter 10. What About the Pastor?

1. Celia Allison Hahn, *Growing In Authority—Relinquishing Control: A New Approach to Faithful Leadership* (Bethesda: Alban Institute, 1994).
2. Moe, *Pastor's Survival Manual*, 77.

Chapter 12. If You Are Wounded

1. Frank Martin, *War in the Pews: A Foxhole Guide to Surviving Church Conflict* (Downers Grove, Ill.: InterVarsity, 1995), 55.
2. *Weavings* is published by The Upper Room. Subscriptions may be ordered by writing to *Weavings* at P.O. Box 340009, Nashville, TN 37203-0009
3. Eugene H. Peterson, *The Message: The New Testament Psalms and Proverbs in Contemporary Language* (Colorado Springs: NavPress, 1993), 625.
4. Peterson, *The Message*, 653.
5. Systems theorist Peter L. Steinke discusses differentiation in two books, *How Your Church Family Works: Understanding Congregations as Emotional Systems* (Bethesda: Alban Institute, 1993) and *Healthy Congregations: A Systems Approach* (Bethesda: Alban Institute, 1996). Edwin Friedman, a pioneer in family systems theory, explores differentiation

extensively in *Generation to Generation: Family Process in Church and Synagogue* (New York: Guilford Press, 1985).

6. Ronald W. Richardson, *Creating a Healthier Church: Family Systems Theory, Leadership, and Congregational Life* (Minneapolis: Fortress, 1996), 85.

Chapter 13. The Rewards of Fitness

1. Gaede, Beth Ann, ed., *Congregations Talking about Homosexuality: Dialogue on a Difficult Issue* (Bethesda: Alban Institute, 1998), 114.

Bibliography

Gaede, Beth Ann, ed. *Congregations Talking about Homosexuality: Dialogue on a Difficult Issue.* Bethesda: Alban Institute, 1998.

Gregory, H. William. *Faith Before Faithfulness: Centering the Inclusive Church.* Cleveland: Pilgrim Press, 1992.

Hahn, Celia Allison. *Growing in Authority–Relinquishing Control: A New Approach to Faithful Leadership.* Bethesda: Alban Institute, 1994.

Halstead, Kenneth A. *From Stuck to Unstuck: Overcoming Congregational Impasse.* Bethesda: Alban Institute, 1998.

Halverstadt, Hugh F. *Managing Church Conflict.* Louisville: Westminster John Knox, 1991.

Hopkins, Nancy Myer, and Mark Laaser, eds. *Restoring the Soul of a Church: Healing Congregations Wounded by Clergy Sexual Misconduct.* Bethesda: Alban Institute, 1995.

Leas, Speed. *Moving Your Church Through Conflict.* Washington: Alban Institute, 1985.

Leas, Speed, and Paul Kittlaus. *Church Fights: Managing Conflict in the Local Church.* Philadelphia: Westminster, 1973.

Martin, Frank. *War in the Pews: A Foxhole Guide to Surviving Church Conflict.* Downers Grove, Ill.: InterVarsity Press, 1995.

Moe, Kenneth Alan. *The Pastor's Survival Manual.* Bethesda: Alban Institute, 1995.

Norris, Kathleen. *Dakota: A Spiritual Geography.* Boston/New York: Houghton Mifflin, 1993.

———. *Amazing Grace: A Vocabulary of Faith.* New York: Riverhead, 1998.

————. *The Cloister Walk.* New York: Riverhead, 1996.

Olsen, Charles M. *Transforming Church Boards into Communities of Spiritual Leaders.* Bethesda: Alban Institute, 1995.

Oswald, Roy M., and Robert E. Friedrich, Jr. *Discerning Your Congregation's Future: A Strategic and Spiritual Approach.* Bethesda: Alban Institute, 1996.

Oswald, Roy M., and Speed B. Leas. *The Inviting Church: A Study of New Member Assimilation.* Bethesda: Alban Institute, 1987.

Peck, M. Scott. *Golf and the Spirit: Lessons for the Journey.* New York: Harmony Books, 1999.

Peterson, Eugene H. *Working the Angles: The Shape of Pastoral Integrity.* Grand Rapids: Eerdmans, 1987.

Phelps, Joseph. *More Light, Less Heat: How Dialogue Can Transform Christian Conflicts into Growth.* San Francisco: Jossey-Bass, 1999.

Richardson, Ronald W. *Creating a Healthier Church: Family Systems Theory, Leadership and Congregational Life.* Minneapolis: Fortress, 1996

Rilke, Rainer Maria. *Letters to a Young Poet.* New York: Vintage, 1986.

Schaller, Lyle E. *The Interventionist.* Nashville: Abingdon, 1997.

Steinke, Peter L. *Healthy Congregations: A Systems Approach.* Bethesda: Alban Institute, 1996.

————. *How Your Church Family Works: Understanding Congregations as Emotional Systems.* Bethesda: Alban Institute, 1993.

Tannen, Deborah. *The Argument Culture: Moving from Debate to Dialogue.* New York: Random House, 1998.

Willimon, William H. *Preaching about Conflict in the Local Church.* Philadelphia: Westminster, 1987.